ACCESSING
THE *Scriptures*
THROUGH STUDY AND PRAYER

God's Earthly Servants

Cast in God's Divine Drama

FIVE BIBLE WORK STUDIES
FOR - INDIVIDUALS - COUPLES - GROUPS

FROM THE BOOKS OF
JOSHUA, JUDGES,
RUTH, ESTHER, ROMANS

JOHN PENNINGTON
LARGE PRINT BIBLE STUDIES
VOLUME THREE

WESTBOW
PRESS®
A DIVISION OF THOMAS NELSON
& ZONDERVAN

Commentaries
Thru The Bible J. Vernon McGee Thomas Nelson
The Bible Exposition Commentary/Prophets Warren W. Wiersbe Victor/Cook
The Bible Exposition Commentary/New Testament Vol. 2 Warren W. Wiersbe Victor/Cook
The MacArthur Bible Commentary, Unleashing God's Truth, One Verse at a Time
Copyright 2005 by John MacArthur, Printed by Thomas Nelson

WestBow Press books may be ordered through booksellers or by contacting:

WestBow Press
A Division of Thomas Nelson & Zondervan
1663 Liberty Drive
Bloomington, IN 47403
www.westbowpress.com
1 (866) 928-1240

ISBN: 978-1-5127-7996-7 (sc)
ISBN: 978-1-5127-7995-0 (e)

Library of Congress Control Number: 2017904411

Print information available on the last page.

WestBow Press rev. date: 04/04/2017

To my grandchildren,
You are, and were always, in my heart.

Amanda – Joshua – Julia – Kameron – Lane – Skyler

"The lord bless you and keep you,
The Lord make his face shine upon you,
And be gracious to you;
The Lord turn his face toward you
And give you peace."
Number 6:24-25

CONTENTS

Four Lessons from the Book of Joshua (Abridged)

Five Lessons from the Book of Judges (Time before the Monarchy, Abridged)

The Book of Ruth

The Book of Esther

Romans

FROM THE AUTHOR

One new start calls for other new starts!

When was the *last time* you did something for the *first time*? Let me share with you how a progression of doing <u>several somethings for the *first time* changed my life</u>. In fact, my perception and purpose of life changed.

In his book, The Purpose Driven Life, Rick Warren points out that <u>we live for God's pleasure</u>. Being raised apart from the Church, I assumed our purpose on earth was to be law-abiding and please ourselves as much as our income would allow. As a young family man, I joined a church for the *first time*. Certainly a good start! But for the next twenty-five years I did *nothing new*. I simply took up space in the same pew. <u>I hadn't even purchased a Bible</u>. I misused the talent God gave me for music by being a music critic during hymn singing rather than lifting my voice to God. Worse, I harbored disparaging thoughts about the poor pitch of the women singing around me including my spouse. There were no men to critique because they, like myself, just stood there like bumps on logs while their wives did the singing. I will admit, peer-pressure was part of the reason for my lack of hymn participation.

For the next two decades I went to church while the kids grew taller. Still *nothing new*! <u>I hadn't purchased a Bible</u> and I remained prayer-less. Having never uttered grace at dinner, I was a spiritual dry hole for those I dined with. I never attended a Bible study. Two gifted pastors served the church we attended, preaching wonderful sermons. But at the end of the day, I still believed our purpose on earth was to be law-abiding and please ourselves as much as our income would allow.

The Spirit's leading is ever present. He is ever speaking to us. The problem is, having the *will* to hear His voice. <u>Doing something for the *first time* is a matter of the *will*</u>. Attending my *first Bible study* led to my *first purchased Bible*. Then the confidence to deliver my *first public prayer* followed. Then came my *first leading a Bible study*. I accepted my *first Teaching Directorship* which led to *writing my first Bible study lesson* and then publishing my *first Bible workbook*. I joined my *first church choir* and later *directed my first church choir*. I now sing with joy in our Sanctuary Choir. I am no longer the music critic acknowledged in an earlier paragraph.

Doing something for the first time changed my life. It certainly did the individuals God used that you will meet in the foregoing studies. Do something for the first time! <u>Form a small group and welcome friends to a new Bible study</u>.

LOOK IT UP! WRITE IT DOWN!

I spoke of hearing marvelous sermons yet remained biblically illiterate. All of us learned core subjects such as grammar, math, history and biology by means of a pencil and a workbook. I believe heavily, a workbook in combination with an overview is superior to lecture alone. There is no substitute for cementing information than to look it up and write it down! And, a workbook affords the opportunity for interactive discussion. It is amazing how much we learn from others.

Do older adults want to go back to school and prepare lessons? NO! Now you know why I prepare the workbooks we use. The pedagogy, and this is important, for a residential Bible study *must fit* to keep the group returning year after year. We briefly tried studies that provide answers in the back of the book but found they discouraged discussion and required little in the way of looking up related Scripture. Looking up Scripture is invaluable to discovering the geography of your Bible.

A pastor once told me, a study that does not require some page turning is too dumbed down to be of much value. Even though these studies are relatively brief, they require examining other parts of your Bible apart from the subject being studied.

NEVER CEASE LEARNING

"Ask and it will be given to you;
seek and you will find;
knock and the door will be opened to you."
Matthew 7:7

This verse is my favorite to encourage people to attend a Bible study. Like piano lessons, weekly accountability pays dividends.

Some see this verse as relating to necessities. Others errantly relate the verse to God being a vending machine dispensing material goodies. For me, it is for God to open His Word up to me. Beloved, He has done this for me and our class members. They feel blessed when making new discoveries about God and about themselves.

As you study God's Word, do so with the intent to grow your relationship with your Lord and Savior. For certain, Bible study should never be viewed as a means to earn brownie points with God.

BE A TEACHER

"Do you understand what you are reading, Phillip asked?"
How can I, he said, unless someone explains it to me?"
Acts 8:30

<u>Truly, none of us can pass on information we ourselves do not possess</u>. A young believer often looks to an older believer for clarifications. We either give it to them or we know our way around the Bible to tell them where to look. If a skeptic asks why you believe in Jesus and you reply 'well I just do, this is no witness to the lost! To them, faith and belief are foolishness. Skeptics need reasons and we need to give it to them! Faith is fitting when around other believers. But regarding the lost, we must *be equipped* to know why we have faith. If anyone ever told you faith is blind, they are wrong. <u>Fulfilled prophecy is a reason to believe</u>. Eyewitness accounts of the Apostles is another. Creation is yet another. The writers of the Bible were separated by centuries, yet all point to Christ. Isn't that just simply amazing? Absolutely, faith is on solid ground! To be an effective messenger of Christ requires the principles of Colossians 3:16, 2 Timothy 4:2 and 1 Peter 3:15.

AND FINALLY

Life's path takes many turns. If God has a purpose, sometimes He will relocate you. There are numerous examples in Scripture where God relocated His servants. In my life, biblical literacy was sorely needed. Efficacy to God was a matter of geography, literally. Relocation opened the door for meeting my wife Mary in Albuquerque, New Mexico. She gifted me with a leather-bound Bible with <u>my name etched on the cover</u>. A feeling came over me that I had never experienced. It was as if viewing my name written in the Lamb's Book of Life! I was charged to do something with it!

But who would teach me? There was an Ethiopian of Acts 8 who needed Phillip to get him up to speed. At Mary's insistence, we attended a Tuesday night Bible study. It was a first for me. There I met a man who would indeed be my Phillip. He was a godly man named Bob Jefferson, a learned lay leader and Teaching Director of a Community Bible Study in Albuquerque. Subsequently, the enlightenment I came to, God blessed me opportunity to share with others in our community in the coming years. Perfidious spirits prohibited extending this down to include my grandchildren. It is to my grandchildren this book is dedicated.

Give the gift of a Bible to someone.
Inscribe their name on it.
Some will be offended,
But no matter,
You may save a soul.

ACKNOWLEDGMENTS

For a Longsuffering Creator, full of Patience and generous of Grace. For Bob Jefferson, a godly man and gifted CBS Teaching Director whom God placed along my path. The men and women of Heritage Ranch and Villas in the Park communities of Fairview Texas who faithfully attended Tuesday night Bible study classes my wife and I established. And finally, my loving and supportive wife Mary, who began my personal journey to scriptural literacy by literally forcing me to attend a CBS Bible study. Always at my side, she is the spark for every class meeting. Without her set of eyes and able grammatical skills, there would be no end to my run-on-sentences. For the commentaries of gifted men and women whom God granted so much insight. And the Word itself; it is the teacher's teacher.

I mustn't forget music and all who make worship music available. Being a music person, we begin each class with music to set the tone from the toils of the day. We end each class singing "As We Go." This soft and gentle song is a beautiful way to end a Bible study. It is published by LifeWay Press.

These studies were prepared by a lay person for general enlightenment. They will not require the preparation time rigorous in depth studies demand..... John Pennington

Because of where Jesus is today, you have a hope for tomorrow

Jesus is,
God Invisible now seen by men.
Savior, Teacher, and Friend.
King of Kings and Lord of Lords.
Come, bow thy knee.

As Mary and I walked the stone paths of the Via De La Rosa in November 2013 we both remained quiet, at times tearful. We had just come from the Mount of Olives, the Garden of Gethsemane and entered Jerusalem's old city through the Joppa Gate. We had stood at the place where the night before He was crucified, Jesus prayed, anticipated, and resigned Himself to His mission and His purpose. In love, He would give Himself up for us, submitting to being nailed to a tree! By His sacrifice our sins are forgiven. Through Him, all who receive Him are forever reconciled to the Father.

With its shops and barking street vendors, the Via De La Rosa is quite different than in Jesus' day. To walk where Jesus walked is added strength to walk as Jesus taught.

To love one another. Within the walls of the Church of the Holy Sepulcher one gets a surreal sense of what happened here. Events forever changing the world and the destiny of those who love the Lord above all. This is the First Commandment. If you have not studied about the Lord Jesus, do so without delay! He is your Savior, He is your Friend. Let Him also be your Teacher. He will teach you by the only means available, the Bible. If no group is available, form one. Two or three people are all you need, don't delay, bow thy knee. He is King of Kings and Lord of Lords.

"For God so loved the world that He gave His only Son. That who so ever would believe on Him shall have ever lasting life." (John 3:16)

HOW GREAT THOU ART

FOREWORD

From thirty-seven thousand miles away, Apollo 17 astronaut Eugene Cernan snapped this remarkable picture of the earth suspended in space. The picture affirms the words of the Apostle Paul; *"For since the creation of the world, God's invisible qualities - His eternal power and divine nature have been clearly seen."* In regard to the coming Judgment and unbelieving men, Paul writes; *"being understood from what has been made, men are without excuse."* Romans 1:20

From Cernan's photo, it is inconceivable that a creator is not behind such a fantastic physical fact. To believe the earth, its properties and the millions of life forms living on this celestial body is the result of random events requires far more faith than does believing a creator exists. Can an atheist travel Cernan's path and still maintain there is no creator? Assuredly, he would have to be mad to view an earth suspended in space, surrounded by millions of celestial bodies and conclude all of this a random accident! *"Where were you when I laid the foundations of the earth?"* (Job 38:4)

As assuredly as God exists, would He not also communicate with those who were made in His Image? *"So God created man in His own image, in the image of God He created him; male and female He created them."* (Genesis 1:27) One would think that a being who could create from nothingness all that is, men would hunger to hear what He has to say. Sadly, this is not the case. Most people are too caught up with themselves to have any desire to have interest even in this Being who has put on display His magnificence!

By your study of the Bible you have said, "I acknowledge God is real and I want to know the mind of my glorious Creator." For if I know His mind, I will better know Him.

One who loves the Lord is truly Sanctified
One who loves the Lord prays for wisdom, strength and vision
He trust God for every need, every decision.

THE BIBLE

This book contains the mind of God, the state of man, the way of salvation, the doom of sinners, and the happiness of believers.

Its doctrines are holy, its precepts are binding, its histories are true, and its decisions are immutable.

Read it to be wise, believe in it to be safe, and practice it to be holy.

It contains light to direct you, food to support you and comfort to cheer you.

It is the traveler's map, the pilgrim's staff, the pilot's compass, the soldier's sword, and the Christian's charter.

Here paradise is restored, heaven opened, and the gates of hell disclosed.

Christ is its grand object; our good its design; and the glory of God, its end.

It should fill the memory, rule the heart, and guide the feet.

Read it slowly, frequently, and prayerfully.

It is a mine of wealth, a paradise of glory, and a river of pleasure.

It is given you in life, will be opened in the Judgment, and be remembered forever.

It involves the highest responsibility, will reward the greatest labor, and will condemn all who trifle with its sacred contents. Middletown Bible Church

Keys to Successful Study

Understand that from the story being told a principal(s) is being taught:

1. Underline key verses.
2. Circle key words.
3. Where and when the story takes place.
4. Picture yourself present!
5. Who is speaking and to whom?
6. What is the one speaking describing?
7. What or why is the person speaking?

Most mistakes for misunderstanding Scripture are due to not being aware of the context in which the speaker is referring to. It is always a good idea to examine preceding verses, even referring back to the beginning of a chapter.

USING THESE STUDIES

These studies are designed for small groups of likeminded people meeting weekly at the same time and location. The large print makes them advantageous for senior communities. The lessons are useful for individual, couple or family study and are easily understood by those with little to moderate knowledge of the Bible. If you have never attended a Bible study, these studies are for you!

Leading the studies is successful by one person or a couple. Leaders with limited preparation or knowledge should use the 'Helicopter Overview' following the discussion questions. For those living in a restricted community such as senior living or gated HOA, it is recommended a resident serve as leader. Non-resident leaders, even if seminary trained are discouraged! The most well intended non-resident in time becomes inconsistent with outside conflicts as class after class is canceled. Soon, the group dissipates or a resident must step up and lead to save the class anyway. Do occasionally invite a seminary trained guest speaker.

The studies were prepared by a lay person and can be led by an untrained believer willing to serve! Recall, not one Disciple Jesus called was qualified. Yet no one today disputes the statement of the Apostle's Creed. The Word is the real teacher! God didn't call the qualified, He qualified the called! God equips His people! These studies have been successfully tested using lay leaders for ten years. No one ever indicated anything other than, how much they had grown in their knowledge of God.

Rotating leaders is acceptable in the beginning until it is clear one person or a couple are gifted facilitators. Dependable leaders with people skills makes a class go. Ultimately Scripture does the teaching.

The studies are drawn from the NIV Bible. In a class, read only the chapter being studied. [Also read aloud bracketed verses]. Reference verses apart from the study need not be read. Involve everyone in reading! To keep things moving, [bracketed verses] are best read by one person who has them located ahead of time. Occasionally you will find **'TIME OUT'** sections that extend beyond the chapter being studied.

These studies are not intended to make one a biblical scholar but rather, to develop a loving relationship with Jesus. God's Grace in Christ is not fully appreciated until His Word is studied. If your lack of knowledge embarrasses you, get over it and get started! One day you will leave this life. Don't let that day descend on you without fully knowing your Lord and Savior. Know more today about Jesus then you knew yesterday. As your knowledge of Him increases, so shall your love for Him Grow.

THE PRINCIPALS

Joshua

Rahab

Deborah

Gideon

Ruth

Boaz

Naomi

Sampson

Esther

Paul

Four Lessons
The Book of Joshua

Abridged

Setting the Stage for Joshua

"As for me and my house, we will serve the Lord," (Joshua 24:15) It seems a shame that our knowledge of Joshua is centered on this one verse and the walls of Jericho. The same can be said of Jonah and a few others. Most only know of Jonah being associated with a whale and not much else.

God uses Joshua in many ways. First Joshua is the catalyst for the existence of the State of Israel from whence the Christ would come. Second, through Joshua, God demonstrates His Sovereignty over nations. And most importantly for you and me, the nation Joshua establishes is instrumental in God's grand plan of redemption. It is also here in the Book of Joshua, the curse of Anti-Semitism is born. Disdain for the Jew today can be traced back to the time of Joshua.

In this study you will encounter more tribal names than can be remembered. They appear simply to give credibility to Scriptural linage. So don't become frustrated by believing you have to memorize all of the names, you don't!

Now Moses had died. (Deuteronomy 34:5-8) Of the original tens of thousands of Hebrews who had left Egypt forty years earlier, only Joshua and Caleb remain from their generation. The focus in this study is an account of those born during the forty years of wandering. That would make <u>all the males fighting age</u>.

Coming from east of the Jordan, the Hebrews would cross the Jordan and proceed west into the land promised to Abraham, Isaac and Jacob. (Genesis 12:1-3, Deuteronomy 34:4) Joshua is now God's man and he has the daunting task of repossessing land immoral idol worshiping men had claimed for themselves. Conflict, obedience and testing is on the horizon.

And now, the ethical question of war. Because many Christians are repulsed by war, they choose to limit their biblical knowledge to the Gospels and the Epistles. Even the Book of Revelation causes indigestion for some. Beloved, how can one ever come to grips with the hard reality of sin and rebellion against God if we limit our Bible study to the warm fuzzy parts of Scripture? Joshua is textbook reality that before the purity of God's Kingdom can be realized, the <u>Kingdom first has to be purged of the enemies of God</u>. (See Leviticus 18:30) God raises up Joshua for this purpose.

Therefore, the conquest of Canaan has apocalyptic overtones. How so we might ask? The conquest of Canaan by God's people serves notice that <u>earth belongs to God</u>. (Exodus 19:5) Earth was created to be inhabited by those who acknowledge Him and no one else. The first two Commandments make that clear. Those who oppose Him will claim no inheritance. God's entitlement to earth and specifically Israel begins with war against people who did not acknowledge Him. And it will end with war over the whole earth against the same kinds of people. (Revelation 16:16, 19:19)

War is a terrible curse, but the human race brings it on themselves by desiring to possess the earth for their own unrighteous ways. But as horrific as war is, it is pale to the curse that awaits all who reject the Creator's offer of Grace in Christ Jesus.

In this study, you will discover Joshua as both a military leader and a spiritual leader for his people. But the key to his success was not his persona, but his submission to the Lord. Whenever God spoke, Joshua listened and <u>obeyed</u>. Like Daniel in many respects, Joshua is a model for all Christians.

Joshua moved about the land ridding it of its wickedness and idolatress practices. The manner in which Joshua moved in Canaan is a model and motivation for us to move in our own lives to rid ourselves of sins that have setup shop.

Joshua 1-5
God Calls Joshua

Moses has died. Certainly his life was extraordinary. God's Divine plan beginning with Abraham worked its way through Moses and now continues through Joshua. Coming out of Egypt, the Hebrew people had been on the defensive. Now they go on the offense.

Read Joshua: 1:1-9, 16-18

1) *"In the beginning God created the heaven and the earth."* (Genesis 1:1) Land created by God had come to be used by people who honored idols rather than the Creator. Joshua is given the task of repossessing this land for God's Covenant People.

   a. What is God's promise to Joshua?

   b. What is required of Joshua?

   c. Select three truths most apparent here?

   <u>That God is organized</u>   <u>That God Exists</u>   <u>That God is Sovereign</u>

   <u>That God is faithful</u>   <u>Some men are natural born leaders</u>

2) Explain the oath taken by the officers who would serve under Joshua. (v. 17)

Read Joshua 2:1-14, 23-24

3) Canaan was an immoral land, so it is no surprise its king had knowledge of the prostitute Rahab. What plan did this unchaste woman make with the two spies?

Discussion:

Rahab's lie served God's purpose. In light of the teachings of Scripture, how do you reconcile Rahab's lie? Regardless of the circumstances, is lying always sinful?

4) Why were the two spies confident that Jericho would fall to Joshua's army? (v. 24)

Read Joshua 3:2-4, 7, 9-11, 15-17   Preparation for Battle

5) What orders did the Hebrew officers issue throughout the Hebrew camp? (vv. 3-4)

6) Read 1 Peter 5:8 and Job 1:6-7 and identify the enemy we must be on guard for.

7) How do we, in New Testament times, prepare for battles? See Ephesians 6:10-18

8) What is God's message to Joshua? (v. 7)

9) For those who walk in the ways of the Lord, what are they assured of? (v. 11)

10) a. From verses fifteen through seventeen, what event occurs that has occurred before? See Exodus 14:21-22

   b. What do you draw from these events?

Read Joshua 4:1-7, 12-14, 20-24   Spiritual Awareness
11) What was done to remind the Hebrew people who protected them? (v. 3)

12) What necessary step was taken for the army of God to remain unified? (v. 14)

Read Joshua 5:1-8, 13-15
13) What news reached the pagan kings west of the Jordan? How were they affected?

14) Why must circumcision be performed before the siege of Jericho?

Discussion:

What might we consider about the man with a sword? (v. 13) Consider, Joshua is the commander yet he addresses this man as *my Lord*. Joshua also refers to himself as this man's servant!

Author's Note: Joshua can be assured the armies of Heaven are committed to purifying the land for God's Covenant People. So it is not surprising, the armies of Heaven will be committed to purifying the whole earth for His Eternal Kingdom. (Revelation 19:11-16)

15) Compare verse fifteen with Exodus 3:4-5. Why would Joshua remove his sandals?

Summary Statement:

God prepares Joshua to engage Jericho just as He prepared Moses to engage the Egyptian Pharaoh. Joshua's preparation involved both military and Spiritual readiness. Joshua's question in 5:13-14 may be surprising to believers today, considering the answer he receives. *"Are you for us or for our enemies? Neither!"* (Joshua 5:13-14) This is a brief but necessary posturing narrative indicating that God is the One who is in charge. God's Sovereignty is firmly established here in Joshua.

The ethical question of war and the Christian Faith is on trial for those who point out that God is a perpetrator of war. After all, the land God promised Abraham, Isaac and Jacob was already occupied. But beloved, let us not forget, <u>God created the land</u>. Certainly He didn't create the land to be used by people to worship anything or anyone other than Himself. A God who is Holy and Just will not permit wickedness, debauchery or the worshiping of idols to continue unabated. <u>What Joshua is about to embark on is not war, but Judgment</u>! This Judgment is no different than the Flood, Egypt, and the cities of Sodom and Gomorrah. God eventually brought Judgment on His own people after they too, engaged in wickedness, debauchery and idolatry. The final Judgment revealed in the Book of Revelation will be for these same reasons. *"You shall not make for yourself an idol in any form. You shall not bow down to them or worship them; for I, the Lord your God, am a jealous God."* (Exodus 20:5)

When God gives a land to his people, He intends to purify it! The Seal, Trumpet and Bowl Judgments of the Book of Revelation testify to this truth. Before the meek will inherit the earth, God will purify it. Therefore, what is about to happen in Canaan can be paralleled to The Book of Revelation.

The account of the harlot Rahab and the two spies is a testimony that our God is merciful, whatever their station, to those who acknowledge Him. Which brings us to the narrative about the twelve stones. The stones have no power but they do serve to <u>remind coming generations</u> of God's love for His people. He looks after the needs of His people. Certainly God looked after our needs when He sent His Son into the world to give Himself for our sin. What stones served in that day, the cross serves today. The stones (and the Cross) are reminders to acknowledge God and be obedient to His laws. The Redemption of Rahab extending to her entire family demonstrates the impact just one redeemed person can have on other lost family members.

Application

What a chain of events! Seize every opportunity to serve the Lord. Joshua had an opportunity to serve the Lord and he did. The two spies had the opportunity to serve the Lord and they did. Even Rahab, a prostitute, served the Lord. Beloved, let us never grow too old, be too busy or feel too unworthy, to serve the Lord.

If you are one who has yet to receive Jesus, do so now. Accept Jesus as your Lord and Savior this very moment. *"Here I am! I stand at the door and knock. If anyone hears my voice and opens the door, I will come in and eat with him, and he with me."* (Revelation 3:20) Now go. Serve the Lord.

Notes for Joshua 1-5

Joshua 6-12
Conquest of Canaan

"For the sin of the Amorites has not yet reached its full measure." (Genesis 15:16) Evidentially, by the time we get to the time of Joshua, the full measure of detestable practices by the pagan Amorites, Canaanites and numerous other cultures located here were pervasive. A reading of Deuteronomy 18:9-12 should put to rest any thought that we might question God precipitating Judgment over this Land. Canaan, a land promised to Abraham, was not in its current state, fit to be a gift to God's people.

Read Joshua 6:1-5, 15-19

1) What did God tell Joshua to have the people do on the seventh day? (v. 5, 16)

2) All the inhabitants of Jericho were put to the sword except one family. Who was spared and why? (v. 17) See also Hebrews 11:31

3) In the New Testament, how would someone such as Rahab be at peace with God? See Romans 5:1

Read Joshua 7:1-4, 11, 20-25

4) What was the sin that angered the Lord?

5) What happened when the Hebrews attacked at Ai?

6) What happened to those who angered the Lord? (v. 25)

Discussion:

The sin of Achan and others affects the whole camp. This remains true today. The sin of a few, even of one person, affects other people. What are ways sin affects our personal contacts? What are ways society is affected by the sins of a few?

Read Joshua 8:1-4, 10-19, 31-32

7) With everything of Achan removed, Israel was cleansed of any disobedience. The Lord was again with Joshua and the Hebrews. After one failed attack against Ai, what was the result of the second attack?

8) After Ai was taken, what did Joshua do? (vv. 31-32)

9) How might you and I today respond to what Joshua did on Mount Ebal? See Hebrews 10:16 and Romans 12:1-2

*Optional Reading: Joshua 9

Read Joshua 10:1-13

10) How does Joshua 10:1-13 relate to Romans 8:28-31?

Read Joshua 11:1-9, 16-23

11) With God with them, how well did Joshua and his men fare in clearing the land of idol worshiping pagans?

Discussion:

Do you have any reservations about God leading Joshua to inflict such carnage upon so many people? How do you explain the necessity of the death of so many people?

Are you aware, religious cleansing is with us today around the world, even against Christians? What is your view of the religious cleansing taking place in Canaan?

12) Compare Joshua 11:20 with Exodus 9:13-16. Why did God harden the hearts of certain men?

13) In relation to the Jordan and the Mediterranean, which side of the Jordan would Joshua now be in control? (Joshua 12:7) Locate on a map if one is available.

Summary Statement:

Enroot too many military successes, one act of disobedience momentarily derailed Joshua and his men. That sin was atoned for and Joshua was victorious for the Lord.

 **Leader's Helicopter Overview of Joshua 6-12**
(Optional or Prepare Your Own)

Deuteronomy 12:29-31, 18:9-14 and Leviticus 18:21 reveal the Old Testament's most <u>vivid and detestable accounts of pagan practices and worship</u> in Canaan. The Lord would have no more of it. This lesson cannot be fully understood without reading these torrid scriptural accounts.

God's cleansing of Canaan is a precursor to Revelation 6-19. Canaan was not a fit place for God's Holy people to live in. And so it will be at the end of the ages, the earth will not be a fit place for Christ and His Bride. John's Revelation at the end of the Bible makes clear, the whole of the earth will be purified and made ready for a Holy People. As it was with the Canaanites, so shall it be at the end of the ages. All who live apart from God will have no place in His dominion.

We see here in Joshua further evidence God is in control. In today's world men think they are in control but they are foolishly mistaken. Flesh gives way to dust, but the Spirit remains forever.

This overview is deliberately shortened to allow time to <u>read the suggested Scriptures</u>. Please do so.

Application

Chapter seven sends home the message that sin affects not only the perpetrators, it affects the whole community of God's people. Christians are a people set apart to be honorable, trustworthy and obedient to all of God's Law. We are made for worship; one God, one Christ, one Spirit, one Creator of all that is.

"Shout to the Lord all the earth. Worship the Lord with gladness,
Come before him with joyful songs. Know that the Lord is God.
It is he who made us, and we are his, we are his people, the sheep of his pasture.
Enter his gates with thanksgiving and his courts with praise;
Give thanks to him and praise his name. For the Lord is good and his love
Endures forever; His faithfulness continues through all generations."
Psalm 100

Notes for Joshua 6-12

Joshua 13-21
Division of Land by Tribes

Years have passed and Joshua is much older now. Over his lifetime, God used Joshua to defeat thirty plus pagan kings but still, pockets of idolatress societies remained. One of those societies are the Philistines whom we shall see again.

Joshua had established enough of a toe hold in the land that it was now feasible to parcel out sections of land to the tribes of the Hebrews. Again, God is in control of the division of these lands with Joshua serving as the administrator.

Read Joshua 13:1-8

1) Joshua had conquered much, but challenges remain. Since Joshua was advanced in age, what was God's promise to him? **(v. 6)**

2) Who had been God's agent to assign land east of the Jordan? (v. 8)

3) How many kings had Moses and the Hebrews defeated east of the Jordan?
See Joshua 12:1-6

4) Briefly scan Joshua 14 through 19 and count the number of tribes to occupy land west of the Jordan (present day Israel) portioned off to them.

5) What was different about the Tribe of Manasseh? (v. 6) See also Deuteronomy 3:13

6) Explain why the Tribe of Levi was omitted from being given land. See Deuteronomy 18:1-8

7) The assignments of lands was not happen-chance. Using one example to illustrate this truth, when and who determined the land Caleb would receive? See Numbers 14:24 and Deuteronomy 1:34-36

Read Joshua 20:1-9

8) What was the purpose of the city of refuge?

Discussion:

In our modern society, how might people be killed and the one responsible is never charged with a crime? Do you think revenge by friends and family of a loved one is warranted when a no fault death has occurred?

Read Joshua 21:41-45

9) Though the Levites were not allotted a specified area of land, they nevertheless were scattered over all Israel to minister to the people. How many towns did the Levites take up residence in? (v. 41)

10) For Joshua, what was the end result of his efforts of battles fought? (vv. 43-45)

11) a. What had been God's promise to Abraham? See Genesis 12:2-3

   b. What was Abrahams response to what the Lord had asked of him?

Summary Statement:

Joshua didn't just settle for Jericho. He kept on keeping on. For this reason, God was with him to the end of his life. *"The Lord gave them rest on every side."* (Joshua 21:44)

If we were to research the assignments of the lands to the tribes of the Hebrews we would find this wasn't randomly determined by Joshua. These assignments were meticulously parceled out by the Lord who already foreknew who would get what even during the desert wanderings.

For example, Caleb was predetermined to possess the land he had set foot in when serving as a spy. (Numbers 14:24, Deuteronomy 1:34-36) His spy report had pleased the Lord because the <u>report was not one of gloom and doom, but rather one of optimism</u>.

Author's Note: Well try telling that to some of today's gloom and doom media sources. Amazingly, some are Christian. Christian or not, they are so contrary to God's Word, it boggles the mind the number of Christians listening to them. They are clouds without rain. Assuredly, they have an agenda and it isn't to build you up! (1 John 4:1) Read on why God's people need never live in fear.

<u>Caleb had been optimistic because</u>, unlike the other spies, <u>he was sure in the Lord</u>. Being sure of God's saving Grace in Jesus is one of our lessons here. The other lesson is having full confidence in God's Sovereignty regarding nations and who leads them. The placement of the Tribes of Israel confirms this. For it was at the direction of a Sovereign Creator the Tribes of Israel were stationed.

In the Middle East today, there are nations that simply refuse to acknowledge that Israel exists. Some countries adjoining Israel do not include them on their maps. The conflicts that raged during Joshua and David's time continue today. To put our finger on the why of this, we need only go back to Genesis 15, 16 and 21 and the story of Sarah and Hagar concerning Isaac, the child of promise, and Ishmael.

We need not remember the details of names and principalities named in chapters twelve and thirteen, but it is important to remember why such lists are recorded in a literary work such as the Bible? <u>To give the Bible credibility</u>! To let you and I know that these were actual events, places and people. That none of it is made up. There are no fairy tales here. These lists assures us the Bible is not a piece of fiction, not one word of it. <u>That is why the Gospel of Jesus Christ is so believable.</u>

Couple the historical information contained in the Bible and the fulfilled prophecies of the Prophets such as Isaiah concerning Christ, there is only one conclusion, the Bible is the indisputable Word of God. No mortal or group of mortals could have collaborated over centuries to generate to the last detail such minute information.

Joshua's generation found rest in the Lord. But succeeding generations would not fare as well because they began falling away into apostasy and disobedience.

Application

Keep on keeping on. Like Joshua and Daniel years later, once you have entered the Lord's service, <u>never quit</u>. It is not enough to witness to a lost soul. For when that soul is won for Christ, <u>another lost soul is waiting</u> in the wings for your testimony.

"The Lord gave them rest on every side." (Joshua 21:44) The people of Joshua's generation had no worries from their enemies. We have that same promise today. *"Therefore, since the promise of entering his rest still stands, let us be careful that none of you be found to have fallen short of it. For we have also had God's Grace preached to us."* (Hebrews 4:1-2)

Notes for Joshua 13-21

Accessing the Scriptures

Joshua 22-24
Remember God's Goodness and Mercy

As a result of God's mercy, the Hebrews are firmly in control of the West Bank side of the Jordan. A time of rest and Spiritual reflection has come to what must surely be a weary people. In due course, the Reubenites, Gadites and the half-Tribe of Manasseh returned back to the east side of the Jordan. In time, this would become problematic.

Read Joshua 22:1-8

1) What was the mood of the tribes who would be returning back to their homes east of the Jordan?

2) a. What pointed instructions did Joshua give to those who were returning to the east of the Jordan? (v. 5)

   b. Regarding verse five, do you think Jesus made the Law of Moses invalid?

   c. What actually did Christ do regarding Mosaic Law? See Matthew 5:17-18

3) In regard to selfishness, what was Joshua's instructions to the Reubenites, the Gadites and the half-Tribe of Manasseh? (v. 8)

Read Joshua 22:9-12

4) Regarding the Lord, what honor to the Lord did the two and a half tribes do on the east side of the Jordan where they were to live? (v.10)

5) What was the reaction of the Hebrew Tribes west of the Jordan? (vv. 11-12)

Time Out: West of the Jordan where the Ark of the Covenant was kept, a permanent alter already existed at Shiloh. Sites were already in place west of the Jordan for offerings. These sites were scattered about the newly conquered land to reduce travel. So this altar east of the Jordan was considered to be apostasy. The idea of a religious war was simply a knee-jerk reaction of one brother being upset with a fellow brother.

Read Joshua 22:24-27

6) What was the principle reason these two and a half tribes east of the Jordan built an altar to the Lord?

Read Joshua 23:1-3, 6-16

7) Who does Joshua give the credit to for what the Hebrews have gained?

8) What <u>two principle directives</u> does Joshua give to the Hebrews? (vv. 6-8)

9) What final warning does Joshua give to the Hebrews? (vv. 12-16)

Discussion:

The chaos in the world today does seem confined to countries where Christ is not revered. Certainly what is seen on the news is heart breaking. Still, do you think the tragedy in non-Christian countries is proportional Judgment on unbelieving people?

Read Joshua 24:1-27

10) What is the significance of gathering at Shechem? See Genesis 12:6-7

Discussion:

The reassembling of the Israelites in Shechem at the base of Mt. Ebal we would call a revival today? This location had an effect on the people. What effect might it have on a Christian to visit a Christian book store? How valuable would this be to take one's children? – If you have visited Jerusalem, Galilee or other sites where Jesus ministered, what things came to focus? What things never entered your mind?

11) What is Joshua's central point in his closing dissertation? (vv. 14-15, 19-20)

12) What does Joshua mean when he speaks? *"You are not able to serve the Lord."* (Joshua 24:19) See Proverbs 3:5

Summary Statement:

For now, Israel is at peace. By the mercy of God, they have taken possession of Canaan. Most of the tribes locate west of the Jordan and extend to the Mediterranean. As predetermined, some return to the east of the Jordan. Joshua, now elderly, assembles all Israel at Shechem for a farewell address. Among his final words is this banner in many Christian homes. *"As for me and my house, we will serve the Lord."* (Joshua 24:15) Unfortunately, Joshua's banner would only fly for one generation.

Of all the people who ever lived, Joshua surely is among those who experienced one of the more remarkable lives. As a child, he had witnessed the enslavement of his people at the hand of the Egyptians. He had experienced the desert wanderings and the events that watermark the Book of The Exodus. He was witness to The Shakina Glory, the plagues on Egypt, the parting of the Red Sea, provisions falling from the sky and the giving of the Law. He was witness to the mighty power of God. Most recently he, with Caleb, served as Moses' aide. In his days of leading military campaigns he benefited from a mighty God's intervention. He as much as anyone, knows the depth of the God's Wrath and the infinity of the Lord's Mercy.

The book of Joshua is simply fantastic! To read Joshua and come away with the mind of an atheist, one would have to be mad. The name of every person that appears in Joshua is given credibility by the listing of each person's lineage. There are no made-up fables here.

Something unique has occurred. Certainly God kept His promises. But the people kept their promises. Reuben, Gad and the half-Tribe of Manasseh had kept their promise also. (Numbers 32:25-32) Joshua commends the people for their faithful service. But still, Joshua doesn't rest on the good works of the past. Instead, he reminds the people to be content with what has been allotted them. In other words, don't get greedy and start fighting one another over land. (23.4)

Joshua was indeed a gifted leader with a likeness of David, Daniel and Paul after him. Like them, he credited God with his successes. He issues significant reminders to the people to remain faithful and obedient to the Lord.

Time Out: The faithfulness of Israel lasted only one generation. (1483 B.C.) A reading of Judges 2 reveals, with the next generation, apostasy crept back into Hebrew worship.

There was some concern by those west of the Jordan that the two and a half tribes east of the Jordan had fallen back into idolatry. But that proved to be a baseless kneejerk assumption. Something all of us need to be mindful of from time to time.

Joshua's final address was at a place the Israelites cherished. It befits us at times, to visit special places where only the things of God are present. Alone in a chapel, a Christian book store or perhaps viewing exhibits of Christian art. Certainly a book of Christian reflection and contemplation can serve nicely.

Application

To coin words of one who never quit; *"I have fought the good fight, I have finished the race, I have kept the faith. Now there is instore <u>for me</u> the crown of righteousness, which the Lord, the righteous Judge, will award <u>to me</u> on that day – and not only <u>to me</u>, but also <u>to all</u> who have longed for his appearing."* (2 Timothy 4:7-8)

Like Joshua and scores of faithful men and women like him, keep on keeping on!

Notes for Joshua 22-24

Five Lessons
The Book of *Judges*

Time Before The Monarchy

Abridged

GIDEON SWINGING AX AT ASHARAH POLE

About Judges

If you are looking for moral loveliness in the Bible, Judges isn't the place. In all, God raised up fourteen Judges (deliverers) during the four-hundred fifty year period between Joshua and King Saul. Thirteen Judges appear in the Book of Judges. Some overlap each other's tenure while at other times, gaps of time exist between them.

The fourteenth and final Judge, Samuel, appears in First Samuel. All of these men and one women, Deborah, are God's choice because of two things, they acknowledged Yahweh alone and were people of action.

The Hebrews suffered both external and internal violence from marauding bullies. A type of human pestilence the world won't rid itself of until Christ returns and casts the lot of them into the lake of fire. (Revelation 20:11-15) Maranatha!

The time period for Judges is debated. To get a general idea we place a date of 1480 B.C... to 1030 B. C... or four-hundred fifty years. *"In those days Israel had no king, everyone did as he saw fit."* (Judges 21:25) This final verse of the book sums up Israel's four plus centuries of spiritual apostasy.

Judges is a continuation of the unfolding story of the birth pangs of a nation. <u>God is the loving father who assists in tasks a child cannot complete alone</u>. Time and again it is a story of a Father's discipline followed by His Mercy. For Israel, it was the worst of times, especially spiritually. They had fallen into idolatry, debauchery and all manner of evil doings modeled after the pagan cultures they had inter-mixed with.

Be amazed as you examine conversations and events recorded in such detail. This indicates one thing, a Divine Author: Ancient words, yet relevant for today's world.

Chapter 1 is an account of the ongoing military campaigns following the time of Joshua and the relocation of the two and one-half tribes east of the Jordan. Each tribe was pretty much left to themselves to extract their enemies from the land. Occasionally they helped one another in some of the battles. Since there are no Judges raised up in the chapter, our study will begin with Chapter 2. Chapter 1 does offer up this lesson. If we don't make a successful effort to defeat our enemies, eventually they will defeat us. We of course, are speaking of personal sin that for whatever reason, we never extract from our lives.

Judges 2-3:15
A Backsliding People

The Book of Judges was written several hundred years after the events by Samuel or perhaps others during the time Kings ruled. (Judges 17:6, 18:1, 19:1, 21:25) Israel's lingering animosities with pagan enemies were briefly dormant for the generation of elders following Joshua. But after this faithful generation passed, problems quickly surface, as succeeding generations fall into spiritual malaise compounded by apostasy.

It is obvious from the opening of this chapter, not only have the Israelites forgotten Joshua and the elders following after his time, they had also forgotten the Lord.

Read Judges 2

1) How many times does the word *I* or *me* appear in the first three verses? _____

2) Keeping in mind, the accounts of Judges were written by Samuel or other persons hundreds of years later, (Compare Judges 2:6-9 with Joshua 24:28-30) explain how a writer could write with such detail even the conversations that had taken place?

3) Many, perhaps most people, do not believe the Bible. What does the Apostle Paul say about these folks? See 1 Corinthians 1:18-19 and Isaiah 29:14

4) Offer a general summary of what is taking place in the first four verses.

5) a. Using a dictionary, what is an affliction?

   b. Do you think sin is an affliction and if so, how is sin an affliction?

Discussion: Why might some folks not consider sin an affliction?

6) What action did God take to guide the people and how did this work? (vv. 16-19)

7) Do you think God purposely intended to allow some pagan cultures to survive Joshua's armies so as to use them later to both test and correct His people? See Judges 2:20-23

Note: Don't be in a hurry to finish this lesson. To fully grasp the Book of Judges, it is necessary to grab a pencil and sit and read either Leviticus 26 or Deuteronomy 28.

8) How did the people react upon hearing the truth about themselves? (vv. 2:4-5)

Personal Reflection:

The people being admonished here were foolishly weak. But they were not stupid. They could have added to their sin prideful indignation at being exposed. (Evil loves darkness! When exposed, it lashes back like a trapped lion.) Our people here choose repentance. Do we ourselves receive wise correction with a contrite heart! – Keep in mind, Judgment and correction are not the same. *"All Scripture is God-breathed and is <u>useful for teaching, rebuking, correcting</u> and training in righteousness."* (2 Timothy 3:16)

Read Judges 3:1-6

9) Explain why you think God determined it was beneficial for young Hebrews to learn to engage warfare? (vv. 3:1-4)

10) In the sight of God, what really detestable thing did the Israelites do? (vv. 3:5-6)

Discussion:

From crop growing to making babies, Baal was an adaptable god used by the Canaanites and other pagan societies to, in their minds, bring about plentiful crops and manipulate infertility. Do you think drugs and the various karmas of modern society today qualify as being a type of cult? See Deuteronomy 18:10-11

11) Examine Judges 3:7-15 and describe,
   a. the actions of the people
   b. the actions of God

Summary Statement:

The fickleness of the people brings to mind this New Testament verse; *"Then we will no longer be infants, tossed back and forth by every wave, blown here and there by every wind of teaching and by the cunning and craftiness of men in their deceitful scheming."* (Ephesians 4:14)

<u>An inquiring mind wants to know</u>. Is this *"angel of the Lord"* (v. 1) speaking of himself in the first person repeatedly in the opening three verses, the same individual speaking to Joshua leading up to the battle of Jericho?

"Now when Joshua was near Jericho, he looked up and saw a man standing in front of him with a drawn sword in his hand. Joshua went up to him and asked, "Are you for us or for our enemies? "Neither," he replied, "but as commander of the army of the Lord I have now come." Then <u>Joshua fell facedown</u> to the ground in reverence, and asked him, "<u>What message does my Lord have for his servant</u>?" (Joshua 5:13-14)

Joshua's inquiry speaks volumes. For neither men nor angels are to be worshiped. (Acts 10:25-26) (Revelation 22:8-9) *"The commander of the Lord's army replied, "Take off your sandals, for the place where you are standing is holy.""* (Joshua 5:16) John's vision in Revelation 19:11 portrays Jesus leading a great army. Other appearances such as the fourth person standing in the flames of Daniel 3:25 reveals that God was a hands-on custodian in establishing Israel.

Conclusion: The being here is not representative of a created being such as an angel. The Divine is representing Himself! Surely, this is the <u>pre-incarnate Christ.</u> (Christophany) An examination of Judges 6:14-23 and 13:17-23 sheds further light that God is not above taking the form of an angel, which certainly he could do. (Theophany)

Our first nine verses are a general history delivered to what must have been a national gathering of the Tribes of Israel. God reminds the people of His benevolence in the past. Chastisement follows with a heads-up on the consequences of further sin. To their credit, the people do not display prideful indignation at being chastised. <u>They are deeply remorseful</u> but like addicts and abusers, it won't be long before they are back at their old ways again. *"As a dog returns to its vomit, so a fool repeats his folly."* (Proverbs 26:11) Only regeneration can break the bondage of sin! Judges is very repetitive in that; there is a succession of sin, affliction and mercy, over and again.

Where Joshua's final address (Joshua 23-24) was one of commendation, the Lord's discourse here is condemnation. But be clear, Judges is not a time of Judgment upon Israel! <u>Who judges a child</u>? Judgment comes centuries later to a more mature Israel at the hands of the Assyrians and Babylonians. <u>But Judges is certainly a time of admonishment, correction and, do I have your attention?</u>

Judges answers the question why God did not fully eradicate the *promised land* of all salacious cultures. He was going to use them to strengthen the new nation's armies. (They were going to need them) God would be retesting His people's resolve to remain apart from the allure of societies detestable in His sight.

For a time, God withdraws His assistance to protect the Israelites from their enemies.

Indeed, they will reap the consequences of sin. But that doesn't mean the end plan for Israel is changed. It hasn't! Israel will remain the nation through which the light of the world will come when the time is right.

Application:

There is a lesson to be observed here about our own resolve to not be wishy-washy in our walk of faith. Time after time <u>the people fall away</u> and time after time God regathers them. Repeatedly, they call for mercy and each time, God hears their cries. Are there times you should be calling out for mercy?

Notes for Judges 2-3:15

Accessing the Scriptures

Judges 4-5
External Challenges – Deborah

After the death of the third Judge Ehud, the people once again fall away for a time until God raises up a fourth deliverer. Deborah was the fourth and only female Judge of Israel. When God called her up to meet an enemy, she knew exactly whom to call upon and who to trust, a warrior named Barak. Barak was a bit leery and for good reason. The opposing army had <u>nine hundred iron chariots</u>.

Read Judges 4:1-10

1) Identify four things; the pagan society, its king, army commander and length of time the Hebrews were oppressed. (vv. 1-3)

2) Who was Deborah and what were her duties during the twenty year period of oppression by the Canaanites? (vv. 4-5)

Note: Unlike her male counterparts who settled disputes at the city gate, Deborah adjudicated under a date tree. Perhaps in reference to the sweetness of her decisions?

3) What task did the Lord command Barak to *Go* and do? (v. 6)

4) What instruments of battle would Barak wield that was prophesied in the Song of Moses? Refer also to verse sixteen. See Deuteronomy 32:42

5) From verses four through seven, what two actions did Deborah hold?

6) Being a prophet of the Lord, Deborah was given information about the success of a future event. What success did Deborah prophesy? (v. 7)

7) Summarize Barak's attitude regarding the command to go into battle? (vv. 8-9) Consider verse three.

Read Judges 4:12-24

8) Why was Deborah so sure of military success that she would say to Barak; *"This is the day the Lord has given Sisera into your hands"* (Judges 4:14) See Deuteronomy 9:1-3

9) What possibly do you think that the Lord did ahead of Barak's advancing army? See Judges 5:4-5 and Psalm 18:9-14

10) Why did this Canaanite commander Sisera seek refuge in Jael's tent?

11) What happened to Sisera when he went to sleep in Jael's tent?

Discussion:
Do you think that it was only by accident that the Canaanite leader Sisera found his way to Jael's tent? (vv. 4:17-21) See also John 4:4-8

12) Certainly Barak led an army against Sisera's army of Canaanites and killed them all. Then he pursues the Canaanite commander. But in the end, would you award him the Medal of Honor? Name those you think deserve the credit.

Summary Statement:
Years earlier, Joshua's forces had not eliminated the Canaanites from the central plains of Israel north of Jerusalem. God now uses these surviving pagans to afflict the Hebrews until they decide to *cry out for mercy*. Hearing His people's cry for mercy, God raises up Deborah to rescue and restore the people.

Apparently it took twenty years (vv. 3, 6) of Canaanite oppression before the Hebrews *cried out to God* for relief. For in those days of nation building, God was not slow in coming to the aid of His people.

God doesn't speak directly to Barak, even though he was surely the chief military leader at the time. But as is often the case, God uses various third party means of communicating His commands. Here, our communicator is not another man or an angel, but a woman. Most people view only men as prophets but Deborah (there were other women) is one of the more significant prophets in the Bible.

Deborah has to be one of the more amazing women who ever lived. She neither submitted herself to the mores of the society regarding women nor did she submit to being just another of her husband's possessions. At the same time, she didn't deny or resist her position as a wife nor did she draw back from going forth in service of the Lord. The Song of Deborah which comprises all of Chapter 5 gives all credit, glory and praise to God. In The Song of Deborah, *Lord* appears fourteen times.

To be able to lead a people, serve as judge and prophetess, Deborah was surely familiar with the Song of Moses (Deuteronomy 32) as well as Mosaic Law itself. Wow, she was also a song writer. She trusted God fully to see an impossible military operation through to success. The same can't be said of Barak who needed Deborah to hold his hand. Perhaps Barak thought by holding Deborah's hand he was in essence, holding God's hand. As for the actual battle, verse fifteen suggests a supernatural occurrence from heaven. It was only for Barak and his army to chase down and slay Sisera's fleeing army. We see the same supernatural occurrence in the closing two verses of chapter four. (See supporting Scripture to question nine)

Certainly the woman Jael in this story didn't need anyone to hold her hand. She is of the same mind and fabric as Rahab. She obviously is aware of a major military operation against an enemy. An opportunity to assist in the war effort walks right up to her tent. <u>Without hesitation she acts.</u>

Deborah and Jael demonstrate they were strong in the Faith while Barak reveals his faith was weak. But Barak wasn't stupid. He was aware God was with Deborah. That is why he wanted her present.

Application

This story of Deborah and Barak demonstrates two things: God afflicts people (4:1) who ignore Him (In <u>selective areas</u> of their life) – God accomplishes great things with any man or woman <u>willing to be led by Him</u>!

Of the first, just because we are a member of God's family, doesn't mean discipline is withheld. To the contrary, a sanctified person has huge responsibilities in <u>all areas</u> of Christian living. *"For to whom much is given, from him much is required."* (Luke 12:48 NKJV)

Of the second, the key word is *Go.* (vv. 6, 14) God provided the gifting to His two servants and Deborah and Barak provided the *Go.* She knows immediately how to delegate and Barak, though hesitant, does *Go.* God equips each of us in some way. Now it is up to us to discover our gifts, then obediently <u>supply the *Go*</u>!

Notes for Judges 4-5

Judges 6-8
External Challenges – Gideon

Again, Scripture pictures God's people besieged by enemies. And again comes the cry for mercy! As before, at what is surely an assembled gathering, the people are rebuked! These are not the same people of previous gatherings. <u>It is their offspring</u>. Like their parents before them, history has taught them little.

Once more, a pre-incarnate Christ appears. This time in the presence of a less than enthusiastic Gideon, the soon to be fifth deliverer and Judge. *"But Lord," Gideon asked, how can I save Israel? My clan is the weakest in Manasseh, and I am the least in my family."* (Judges 6:15) Doubt gives-way to assurance of victory.

Read Judges 6:1-18

1) Having again committed evil in the eyes of the Lord, how did God afflict the people and for how long? (vv. 1-6)

2) Write a brief comparison of verses seven through ten with Judges 2:1-3.

3) How startled do you think Gideon was when addressed as a mighty warrior? (v. 12)

Note: Imagine yourself on your knees scrubbing the deck of a ship when someone comes up to you and addresses you as - "Admiral, the President of the United States is on the phone and wants you to lead the invasion of Iwo Jima."

4) Briefly describe how Gideon comes across in meeting with the Lord. (vv. 13-15)

5) Surely Gideon was familiar with God's power from history. So why do you think Gideon is unsure of what is being asked of him?

Read Judges 6:25-31, 36-40

6) What specific instructions was Gideon given regarding his father? (vv. 25-26)

7) How did people react to Gideon tearing down his father's alter to Baal? (vv. 29-30)

8) What was Joash's defense of his son tearing down Baal's altar? (v. 31)

9) Compare verses thirty six through forty with Judges 4:8. What similarities does Gideon seem to share with Barak?

Read Judges 7:1-16, 22

10) Gideon was to engage a Midianite army numbering tens of thousands. What was God's purpose to reduce Gideon's army from thousands to just 300 men? (v. 2)

11) What criteria was used to downsize Gideon's fighting unit to 300 men? (vv. 4-7)

12) What amazing conversation did Gideon hear while eavesdropping on the Midianite camp? (vv. 13-15)

13) What did the Lord bring about when Gideon's men sounded trumpets? (v. 22)

Read Judges 8:1, 4-9, 13-17, 22-35

14) Describe the mind-set of the Hebrews who were not at the frontlines of battle.

15) What ill-fated act did Gideon do that was not in the best interest of the people?

16) After emotions cool over being left out of a glorious victory, in the end, what is offered to Gideon that he humbly declines?

17) Who was Abimelech?

Summary Statement:
By the power and work of God, coupled with the willingness of one man dedicated to the Lord, a great oppressor of the Hebrews is put down.

Faith requires questions and certainly Gideon is full of them. So much so, he prevails upon God to confirm Himself twice by use of dew on a floor covering. Our confirmation today is the Word. Yes, we may have questions, but Faith does not include God performing a miracle every time we are to act. If we are equipped from having done some leg work studying Scripture, we can be sure if an action we are in question about is God's will, or simply the will of our own misguided flesh.

On this same subject, Gideon's questioning is compatible with this verse. *"Do not believe every spirit, but test the spirits to see if they are from God."* (1 John 4:1)

Most of us are like Gideon, we see our own weakness and limitations and completely forget the empowerment that is as close as our knees on the floor. Initially, Gideon is unconvinced he can deliver his people. Once convinced, he is relentless. Another man, who after he was convinced, was relentless. This man was the Apostle Paul. God convinced Gideon, Paul and all who serve the Lord by speaking to them. He speaks to us today through His Son, Christ Jesus.

There is a lesson in men like these. Be relentless in the things of God? That is, vigorously pursue the righteousness of God? Are our works and our words moral and ethical? God has not left us to our own power to pursue righteousness. He has given us a Helper, the Spirit of God. *"And I will pray the Father and He will give you another Helper that He may abide with you forever."* (John 14:16 NKJV)

Verses seventeen and eighteen identify the Being as the pre-incarnate Christ. This is no earthly prophet. If we examine the prophets of the Old Testament we find a linage. Here, there is no linage nor does this heavenly being have a name in the manner of Michael or Gabriel. Gideon even addresses this Being as Lord and offers a sacrifice to Him. Lord is reserved for only one person.

At first, the non-involved Hebrews are disgruntled at not sharing in frontline victory. There is a message here. Not all of us can be on the front lines of glory. It is always Christ-like to serve in unnoticeable ways. Some of these disgruntled glory-seeking folks were given the opportunity to provide behind-the-scenes service but their hurt feelings robbed them of God's blessings. Moreover, Gideon inflicted physical harm on them, even killing some. Beloved, God greatly rewards unselfish actions performed behind the scenes of center-stage-glory.

Gideon does some questionable things regarding vengeful acts God did not ask for. Also, his decision to make an image of gold and silver was not in the best interest of the people. Perhaps worse, Gideon has seventy legitimate sons but that isn't enough. Laying with a concubine, he fathers an illegitimate child who will later wreak havoc on the people. His name is Abimelech. We will see more of him in a later lesson. But still, as with David, Gideon is God's man and to Gideon's credit, he knows the Lord is King and so he declines the people's desire to make him king.

Application

Gideon tore down his father's altar to Baal. Are there altars in your life that need tearing down?

Author's Note: In the eyes of those Israelites who worshiped Baal, Gideon's destruction of Baal's alter was a shameful act. So in this case, Gideon was given a derogatory nickname Jerub-Baal or *scumbag* as we would call it. The Bible often attaches nicknames to people. Jacob is referred to at times as *Israel*. Jerub-Baal will appear as a slur-name numerous times going forward in reference to Gideon. The slur-name the unbelieving world today attaches to believers is *bible-thumper*.

Amazing isn't it? Folks who shamefully worship the idols of the world think of those who love the Lord as something less than themselves, beneath them if you will. It inflates their egos. In their minds, they have discovered greater things! About the intellectual elites Scripture reads; *"God chose the foolish to shame the wise."* (1 Corinthians 1:27) Beloved, those who worship created things and not the Creator are the foolish ones. For these lost souls will one day stand *naked and ashamed* before the Lord at the Judgment. (Revelation 20:11-15) If you know such a person, pray that they come to *see the light*.

Notes for Judges 6-8

Judges 13-16
External Challenges – Sampson

Sampson is an example that <u>God does not override free will</u>. Gifting doesn't make people robots. Were Sampson God's robot, he wouldn't have gotten in the mess he did.

Countless instances of consequences suffered by gifted people exist. Freewill boils down to making choices. Sampson is an eye opener to not throw caution to the wind. When we listen to the wrong people, bad things can happen. Sampson demonstrates that being gifted in one area doesn't make up for extreme weaknesses in other areas.

Read Judges 13

1) What is noticeably different about Sampson's appearance in Scripture from that of Gideon, Deborah and other deliverers? **(vv. 3-5)**

2) Compare the similarities and circumstances of Sampson's birth with those of Isaac and Jesus. See Genesis 17:21 and Luke 1:26-32

3) What do Sampson, Samuel and John the Baptist have in common? See 1 Samuel 10-11, Luke 1:16-17 and Numbers 6:1-7

Read Judges 14

4) What was Sampson's request to his parents that pleased them? (vv. 1-3)

5) Might Sampson's request of a Philistinian wife was Divine Providence? (v. 4)

6) What event indicates God had granted Sampson special power? (v. 6)

7) What was the wedding feast riddle with thirty men in reference to? (vv. 6-9)

8) What problem arose as a result of this riddle? (vv. 15-16)

9) Why do you think Sampson hadn't already explained the riddle to his wife?

Discussion:

Sampson's wager with thirty men could prove costly. His weakness for feminine emotion is costly as his wife betrays him. <u>Do you think a spouse who betrays a marital confidence truly values either the marriage or the spouse?</u>

10) Following the debacle of his wager, what sins does Sampson commit? (vv. 19-20)

Read Judges 15

11) These foregoing verses are material suitable for a soap opera. What sins are ongoing that is pretty much summed up in a single verse? (v. 3, 11b)

12) Using God's gift of strength, how long does Sampson keep the Philistines in check? (15:20)

Read Judges 16

13) While Sampson was visiting a prostitute in Gaza, a trap was set to capture him. Instead of capturing him, what did Sampson do to these folk's town? (v. 3)

14) Who is this new Philistine woman Sampson falls in love with? _____ (v. 4)

15) What is Delilah's scheme and what would she be paid? (v. 5)

16) How many times did Sampson give Delilah false information about how his strength could be compromised? _____ (vv. 6-15)

17) What do you conclude when comparing Judges 16:16-17 with Judges 14:16-17?

Self-Examination: How well do you learn from past mistakes? Do you continue to make the same types of mistakes? If so, why do you think you do? What must change?

18) In Sampson's time of trial, where does he direct his attention? _____ (v. 28)

19) What final blow does Sampson inflict on the Philistines and their silly god thing? (vv. 23-24, 29-30)

Summary Statement:

Sampson is not the image of what a total man should be. The strength God gifted him with is totally compromised when he listens to the wrong people. Still, Sampson was God's man at a point in time and God didn't abandon him. The women revealed their character when they revealed trusted information. Neither woman valued Sampson nor did either contribute to his potential.

Sampson's wife didn't recognize what she had in Sampson. For her to reveal trusted information was reprehensible! Delilah betrayed Sampson for personal gain. Beloved, if someone doesn't value you, flee from that relationship. Don't continue investing in it! <u>They are just not that into you</u>. It will save you a lot of trepidation. They may eventually contribute to your death and place the blame on you.

Sampson's tragedy helps us understand why God didn't want his people attaching themselves to godless people. Sampson's parents knew this but they relented. There is a message here for you and me. <u>Do not invest in folks who live only for pleasure and gain</u>. These individuals are always taking but never giving. *"Have nothing to do with the fruitless deeds of darkness, but rather expose them."* (Ephesians 5:11) Those we invest our lives with either restrain potential or assist potential. Christians need to be alert regarding whom they form relationships.

"For what fellowship can light have with darkness?"
2 Corinthians 6:14

As for Sampson, his choices in women didn't serve to elevate him whatsoever. <u>Neither of these women valued their relationship with him</u>. Both undermined him before others. Their relationship with Sampson was simply self-serving. Ironically, God gave both women an opportunity to perhaps be entered in the Book of Hebrew's Hall of Faith. Both women blew it as neither are ever mentioned again in Scripture.

To simply use the lesson here as a reason to not listen to one's spouse <u>misses the whole point</u>. The lesson here is to always look beneath the surface of people with whom we might form a relationship. The wife's betrayal of spousal confidentiality ignites a chain reaction of sin, suffering and death. Sampson robs and murders others. And ultimately the wife herself perishes.

Beloved, if you have a spouse, don't betray confidential matters to close friends or even children. When you do, you display <u>a selfish motive lurking in your heart</u>. If you fall victim to spousal betrayal such as Sampson, respond with taking the high road. Garner your gifts to do something in the service of the Lord. <u>Sampson failed to do this</u>. As a result, he was afflicted. Only at the end, did he serve the Lord.

Application

Accessing our Value to Others

Keeping in mind the two women in Sampson's life, worth does not have to be determined by personal accomplishment. In the eyes of God, <u>assisting others to serve the Lord makes you immeasurably valuable</u>. Likewise, there is no worse failure than to be a stumbling block that impedes another who would otherwise serve the Lord were it not for you.

Therefore, discern who you or what you listen to? If it is a favorite news channel that is more propaganda than anything else, you are a Sampson. This channel is serving its selfish self, mainly its rating base! These are lips seeking itching ears. Regretfully, <u>those weak in the Word fall away into the devil's traps</u>. Often they are motivated to commit unlawful, even heinous acts in the name of God.

Beloved, know your Bible well enough so that you will immediately recognize the devil's workmen massaging the ears of the vulnerable.

Notes for Judges 13-16

Judges 9, 19-21
Internal Challenges – Sin

"In those days Israel had no king; everyone did as he saw fit."

The individuals of this lesson portray the above verse. We begin with Abimelech, the illegitimate son of Gideon. He was a wannabe commando and self-declared king of Israel. His mission, self-adulation! A servant's heart he had not. Nothing short of death would stop his blood-thirsty quest for power.

Read Judges 9:1-7

1) What is Abimelech's rationale concerning himself? (v. 2)

2) How did Abimelech use the funds given him from the pagan god Baal? (v. 4)

3) What heinous act did Abimelech carry out against his seventy half-brothers? (v. 5)

4) Who was the lone survivor of Abimelech's massacre of his own blood kin? _____

Author's Note: Verses nine through fifteen is a parable by Jotham, exposing Abimelech as a fraud. A *Good King* sacrifices something of himself that brings comfort to his subjects. What Abimelech did offer as the parable goes, was as useless as the shade of a thorn bush. The man was a taker, not a giver. Jotham never reappears in Scripture. Another person of the same name does appear years later as one of the kings of Judah.

Read Judges 9:45-57

5) As leader of a group of marauders, describe what might be typical of Abimelech's style of kingship. (vv. 44-45)

6) How is Abimelech killed? (v. 52-52)

7) What actions had God done that eventually brought Abimelech down? (vv. 23)

Adding to Israel's spiritual woes were its very own spiritual leaders. Men whose mission to role model godliness in the manner of Moses and Joshua instead *"did as he saw fit."* One such bad example is an unnamed Levite whose quest to avenge the death of his concubine resulted in a protracted internal civil war. What followed was the death of thousands and cities burned. The offending tribe of Benjamin almost became extinct.

Read as you wish from Judges 19-21 if you wish the full story. Our purpose here is to identify the depravity of men and copious sins they commit with its domino effect.

IN YOUR NOTES SECTION, CRITIQUE THE FOLLOWING PARAPHRASED VERSES, EXPOSING THE TRANGRASSIONS GOD WAS WITNESSING FROM HIS PEOPLE.

I

"Now a Levite who lived in a remote area in the hill country of Ephraim took a concubine from Bethlehem in Judah, but she was unfaithful to him and went back to her father's house in Bethlehem, Judah." (Judges 19:1-2) See Genesis 2:24

Note: The main difference between a wife and a concubine was the right of inheritance of the offspring.

II

"After four months her master went to persuade her to return. He had with him his servant and two donkeys. When her father saw him he gladly welcomed him." "The man left with his two saddled donkeys and his concubine." "Come, let's stop and spend the night." "You are welcome at my house, the old man said." (Judges 19:3-20)

Note: In that time, hospitality to one's guest bordered on fanaticism. (RETAIN THAT THOUGHT... ... ...

III

"Wicked men surrounded the house." "Bring out the man so we can have sex with him." "The owner said to them, No, my friends, don't do this disgraceful thing." "Look, here is my daughter and his concubine, you can use them to do to them whatever you wish. But to this man, don't do such a disgraceful thing." "The man took his concubine outside to them, and they raped and abused her throughout the night." (Judges 19:22-24)

IV

"When the master got up in the morning and opened the door to continue on his way, there lay his concubine." "Get up, let's go." But there was no answer. He put her on his donkey and set out for home. When he reached home, he took a knife and cut up his concubine into twelve parts and sent them into all Israel." (Judges 19:27-29)

V

"Then all the Israelites came out as one man, four hundred thousand soldiers armed with swords. Tell how this awful thing happened. So the Levite said, they raped my concubine and she died. Now, all you Israelites, speak up and give your verdict."
(Judges 20:1-7)

VI

"The men of Israel united as one man sent men throughout the tribe of Benjamin, saying, "What about this awful crime that was committed among you?" Surrender those wicked men so that we can stone them to death." "But the Benjamites would not listen to their fellow Israelites." "At once the Benjamites mobilized twenty-six thousand swordsmen from their towns." (Judges 20:11-15) See Deuteronomy 17:7, 21:21

"Israel, apart from Benjamin, mustered four hundred thousand swordsmen and inquired of God. They said, "who of us shall go first to fight the Benjamites? The Lord replied, Judah shall go first." See Judges 1:1-2 *"The Benjamites came out and cut down twenty-two thousand Israelites that day." "The Israelites wept before the Lord and inquired; "Shall we go again to battle against the Benjamites, our brothers? The Lord answered, "Go against them." The second day the Benjamites cut down eighteen thousand Israelites." "They sat weeping before the Lord. They fasted and presented burnt offerings." "Shall we go up again to battle Benjamin our brothers? The Lord responded, "Go, for tomorrow I will give them into your hands."*
(Judges 20:17-28)

Note: For two days, Jesus of the Tribe of Judah was defeated but on the third day, by the power of God (not men) Jesus was raised victorious!

VII

"On that day twenty-five thousand Benjamite swordsmen fell, but six hundred men fled into the desert where they stayed four months. The men of Israel went back to Benjamin and put all the towns to the sword, including the animals and everything they found. All the towns they set on fire." (Judges 20:46-48)

VIII

"The men of Israel had taken an oath at Mizpah: "Not one of us will give his daughter in marriage to a Benjamite." (Judges 21:1) *"Now the Israelites grieved for their brothers, the Benjamites."* (Judges 21:1, 6)

Author's Note: "Oath at Mizpah" – It should be no surprise these selfish men conveniently bind themselves to an oath construed by another selfish man in regard to women. Recall the Rebekah – Leah debacle at the expense of Jacob was perpetrated by Laban, himself a selfish fraud.

IX

"Which one of the tribes failed to assemble at Mizpah?" They discovered no one from Jabesh Gilead had come." So the assembly sent twelve thousand fighting men to Jabesh Gilead

and put to the sword every male and every woman who was not a virgin. "They found four hundred young women who had never slept with a man and took them. The Benjamites were given the women. But there were not enough for all of them. The people grieved for Benjamin." "The Lord had made a gap in the tribes of Israel." (Judges 21:8-15)

Author's Note: The Lord <u>did not</u> make a gap in the tribes! Why would He do that? Unspiritual people are quick to blame God for their problems rather than their own poor and often sinful choices. Had God purposely made a gap in even one of the tribes, it would be reflected in Revelation Chapter 7. This simply is Old Testament *narcissism.*

X

"We can't give them any of our daughters since we Israelites have taken this oath; "Cursed be anyone who gives a wife to a Benjamite." "But look, there is the annual festival of the Lord in Shiloh." So they instructed the Benjamites, "go hide and when the girls of Shiloh come out dancing, rush and seize a wife from the girls of Shiloh. So that is what the Benjamites did. They returned to their inheritance and rebuilt the towns. In those days Israel had no king; everyone did as he saw fit." Judges 21:18-25)

Discussion:

Given that the Apostle Paul came from the tribe of Benjamin, do you think he would condemn the kidnapping of these women? Does the end always justify the means?

Application

Our world is full of the examples found here. Let us not resemble one of them. Whenever we justify our own sins we most certainly are sure to repeat them again and again. When that happens, our sense of integrity is lost and we don't even realize it. Consistent assembly with like-minded people in concert with daily devotionals grounded on biblical principles is paramount to one's walk of faith. The Apostle Paul offers up this passage. *"Do not put out the Spirit's fire. Test everything."*

(1 Thessalonians 5:19, 21) Testing begins with self.

Notes for Judges 9:9, 19-21

Four Lessons
The Book of

Ruth

THIS STORY TAKES PLACE DURING THE TIME OF JUDGES

Two Women of the Bible

RUTH AWAKENS BOAZ

ESTHER MADE QUEEN

About Ruth

Ruth is one of two books of the Bible exhibiting a woman's name – Ruth and Esther.

One of the little gems of the Bible, Ruth is both <u>a love story</u> and a <u>prophetical look</u> at the New Testament. Boaz, Ruth and Naomi are the preeminent love story that began at the cross and is consummated in the Book of Revelation. Some may not see it that way, but if this is not a foretelling of Israel, Christ and the Church coming together, then the story is little more than a sweet footnote of boy meets girl.

Boaz delivers Ruth and Naomi at a dark hour. So too Christ will deliver Israel and the Church. But *"the first shall be last and the last shall be first."* (Matthew 20:16) The Church will be delivered first at the Rapture. Israel follows at the end of Tribulation. This concept was introduced with Jacob and Esau; Israel and Edom.

Another significance of Ruth, she was the great-grandmother of David. This places her in the lineage of Jesus. Being non-Jewish, this gives Jesus a connection with all the world. Three other women are named in the Messianic line; Tamar, Rahab and Bathsheba. Of these four women, only Ruth lived a life we would consider virtuous.

This story of love, faithfulness and devotion occurred at a time when the society didn't demonstrate any of these traits. In fact, the time of Judges is among the darkest of days for Israel. It is reassuring to know that by the Grace of God, <u>pockets of love, faithfulness and devotion can exist, even in dark days.</u>

> *"Gilead is mine, Manasseh is mine; Ephraim is my helmet; Judah my scepter.*
> *Moab is my washbasin, upon Edom I toss the dust from my sandals."*
> **Psalm 108:8-9**

Moab appears as early as verse two. <u>Moab of the Old Testament is today's apostate humanist society</u>. To put it bluntly, Moab is God's garbage can! For the person who wants out, God gets them out. Some folks, such as Orpah in this story, prefer to live in Moab. And God grants them their wish also! But Naomi makes the path for Ruth, a Moabite, to come in contact with the one who would become Ruth's redeemer.

Great hostility existed between the Israelites and Moabites. The invasion of the Israelites of Moabite lands had never been forgotten. The Hebrews viewed Moabites as a heathen society and no Hebrew should live among them.

Ruth, Naomi and Boaz parallel the few virtuous persons of which Christ speaks to the Church at Sardis. *"Yet you have a few people in Sardis who have not soiled their clothes. They will walk with me, dressed in white for they are worthy."* (Revelation 3:4)

Ruth 1
Love's Decision and Faithfulness

Now a Judaist named Elimelech, his wife Naomi and their two sons leave Judah and *sojourn* east <u>back across</u> the Jordan to more fertile land in Moab. This land *seems* to offer a better life. <u>Instead, it becomes a graveyard</u> for the father and his sons. For Naomi, life indeed is a challenge. <u>She wisely seeks to return to God's</u> land of promise.

Time Out: (Sojourn represents traveling amidst lost people) Some today are like Elimelech. They turn their backs on God's provision and seek ways that lead to death. Be it Cults or worldliness dangling like a carrot, the end result is death. *"The god of this age has blinded the minds of unbelievers, so that they cannot see the light of the gospel of the glory of Christ, who is the image of God."* (2 Corinthians 4:4)

Read Ruth 1-13

1) Why did this Hebrew husband pull up stakes and sojourn east, back across <u>old ground,</u> to live among pagans God adamantly didn't want around His people?

2) What was the name and nationality of Elimelech's wife? _____

3) What does the Bible tell us about Moab and its people? *"Woe to you, O Moab! You are destroyed, O people of Chemosh!"* (Numbers 22:29) See also 1 Kings 11:7,

4) What are the names of the two son's wives? _____ _____

5) After living in Moab ten years, what happened to Elimelech and his two sons?

Discussion:

In our society today, what generally is the relationship between a mother and her daughter-law? Should the man die, what generally happens to mother-daughter-in-law relationships?

6) What information came to Naomi regarding Judah? How did she respond? (vv. 6-7)

7) What advice did Naomi give to Orpah and Ruth? (vv. 8-9)

8) a. Where did Naomi place the blame for losing her husband and sons? (v. 13)

   b. Is Naomi right? Was God to blame for losing her husband and sons? Explain

"Wait upon the Lord; be strong and take heart and wait for the Lord."

(Psalm 27:14)

Author's Note: God had judged Naomi's family demonstrating that the sin of one family member, in this case, Elimelech's lack of faith in God's provision, ultimately affects a whole family. But God's Grace, which is too often not seen by us, is ultimately revealed. This story confirms that when we run ahead of the Lord, we are on our own power.

Read Ruth 1-14-22

9) After Naomi's dissertation on the realities of living the ways of God's people, worshiping and fasting with them, what decision do the two daughters-in-law reach?

10) What words indicate Ruth's intentions? (v. 16)

11) From the end of this same verse, (v. 16) what has Ruth gained by her decision?

12) What was Naomi's reaction to Ruth's insistence? (v. 18)

Discussion:

"The two women went on until they came to Bethlehem." (Ruth 1:19) This is hundreds of miles of desert circa 1320 B.C… If you were in Naomi's shoe s, would you have remained in Moab or would you have made this horrendous trip to return home?

13) What was the reception of the women of Bethlehem upon the arrival of Naomi and Ruth in town? (v. 19)

14) Naomi's explanation to the women of Bethlehem reminds you and me of what New Testament Parable of Jesus? See Luke 15:11-32

15) What does verse twenty-two suggest as to God looking after His people?

16) Orpah chose to remain with the pagan culture she was comfortable with rather than travel the hot sandy desert to a new life. Did she make a wise decision?

Summary Statement:

Freewill is exercised. A Jewish man living in Bethlehem near Jerusalem makes a decision that abundance in a godless land trumps God's provision. Guided by his own instincts, he moves his family to Moab, a land awash in idolatry. The decision costs him his life and the lives of his two sons. But a seemingly sad story ends well, especially for you and me. God, being the power He is, uses this man's poor decision to His own Glory. The larger story of Redemption is rooted in this one small chapter.

In a sense, Elimelech parallels the thinking of Judas. Elimelech walked in the Promised Land and Judas walked with the Promised Redeemer. Foolishly, both walked away from God's Grace and unto death. Many do that today. Christ is within reach but some folks stubbornly prefer the road away from God and face Judgment.

The opening verses portrays abandoning God's provision and sojourning to a *garbage can* is more desirable than going to God in prayer for relief from famine. It is highly likely the famine in Judah is a result of the falling away of God's people.

Our Hebrew family (Principally the husband) determines God's provision (Exodus 33:1-3) is not as good as provisions in Moab. Irregardless of provisions, nowhere in the Old Testament does God desire His people to live among an idol-worshiping society. A reading of Joshua reveals this truth. In fact, Bethlehem means *house of bread* and Judah means *praise*. Indeed, Elimelech is out of the will of God! This doesn't mean Evangelism is not worthy, but Elimelech's motive here is not one of Evangelism.

Remember the Parable of the Prodigal Son? He longed to get away from his father's house of plenty and fill his stomach with the things the flesh craves. Beloved, that is the problems with young folks today. They want something other than God's Word to fill their lives. (I-phone comes to mind) We all know how the prodigal ended up eating with swine. Fortunately for the prodigal, he saw the light before it was too late.

Our story begins with a prodigal family that lost faith. When hard times came, rather than remaining steadfast, they panicked and went their own way. God tested them and they failed. God tests us to day! When He does, rest on these words of assurance. *"I look for your deliverance, O Lord."* (Genesis 19:18) *"Wait for the Lord; be strong and take heart and wait for the Lord."* (Psalm 27:14)

As these chapters unfold, we may seem somewhat astonished that Ruth, a non-Jew displays faithfulness. As for Orpah, her decision to remain in idolatry separates her from God and removes her off the pages of Christian history and into oblivion. Her name is never again remembered. Beloved, that is the way it is going to be for all who turn their backs on God's provision in Christ. *"May they be blotted out of the book of life, and not be listed with the righteous."* (Psalm 69:28)

Application

Where do you seek comfort? We have heard it said, <u>be a Daniel</u>. Might we also <u>be a Ruth</u>? Following the way of God's people could cost you your family! This certainly holds true for Ruth. This happens a lot in countries outside the West. Some may be drawn by the Gospel of Truth but family ties, as with Orpah, are just too much for them to breach. With the use of hyperbole, Jesus makes our need for Him explicitly clear!

"Anyone who loves his father or mother more than me is not worthy of me; anyone who loves his son or daughter more than me is not worthy of me, and anyone who does not take up his cross and follow me is not worthy of me." (Matthew 10:37-38) Is there anything or anyone in your life that comes before the Lord Jesus?

Notes for Ruth I

Ruth 2
Love's Kindness

This chapter begins with Naomi, a Jewess and Ruth, a Moabite tearfully remaining together and journeying to Bethlehem of Judah. Both women are in a stressful circumstance with neither having any means of support. They determine their only hope is for Ruth to submit herself into servanthood. (Make this connection. With Christ our Kinsman-Redeemer, His Bride the Church would submit herself into His service)

Read Ruth 2:1-14

1) Identify the man who was a kinsman of Naomi's deceased husband, Elimelech.

2) What is God's command in Leviticus 19:9-10 regarding a landowner's harvest?

3) From verse four, what do we draw from the exchange between Boaz and his slaves about the character of him and his slaves? See Revelation 14:6, 2 Corinthians 3:2-3

Note: Yes, these are slaves. Slavery in the Old Testament was not sin if it did not involve man stealing. See Deuteronomy 15:12-18, Ephesians 6:9 and Colossians 4:1. People unable to support themselves, voluntarily submitted to a land owner short term to work off debt or long term, if they had no means of support. Still, treatment of slaves was regulated. Paul's writings reveal regulated slavery continued into the New Testament.

Discussion:

If we have no other tool to determine a person's character, how does conversation assist in character determination? What about sly smooth talkers/con artists who pick up on your speech and simply tell you what they know you want to hear?

4) Describe the manner of Boaz in addressing Ruth. (vv. 8-9)

5) How are verses eight and nine suggestive of the person of Jesus?

6) Compare verse eleven with Mark 10:29-30 and Luke 14:26-27

Time Out: *"hate your father and mother."* This is a tall order and what about the Fifth Commandment to honor your father and mother? <u>The Bible cannot contradict itself</u>. Without going into Greek word semantics too deeply here, we consider two possibilities. One: Literary style sometimes uses hyperbole to highlight a point. Second: The Greek word Agape is used here indicating centering on one's will as opposed to emotions. <u>Agape positions God in first position</u>. In the Greek, Agape is never hate.

7) What was Ruth's reply to Boaz after he had spoken so eloquently of her? (v. 13)

Read Ruth 2:15-23

8) What character quality does Ruth reveal about herself in verses fourteen and eighteen?

9) From verses fourteen through sixteen, what do you observe about Boaz's emotions regarding Ruth?

10) What kind of accolade did Naomi give Boaz? (v. 20)

11) What arrangement did Boaz make to protect Ruth from possible harm during periods of gleaning? (vv. 21-23)

12) Examine verses twenty two and twenty three carefully. Do you see the warning that relates to the dangerous Religious Cults of today? Explain:

Summary Statement:
Boaz is immediately smitten with Ruth and Ruth is obviously delighted as she excitedly relates to Naomi her meeting with Boaz.

To Naomi's credit, after the death of her husband and only means of support, she saw no hope among the idol worshiping society in Moab. Wisely, she makes the decision to return to Bethlehem and the land God had given to the Patriarchs of her people. The hot sandy journey wouldn't be easy but still, <u>it offered hope</u>. By her action, Naomi displays her faith. Accompanying her will be Ruth, one of her two daughters-in-law. Ruth's decision to go with Naomi displayed everything the Church is called to display today; devotion, faith, hope and love. From a New Testament perspective, Israel (Naomi) is going to be the means to Salvation for the Church (Ruth) and the Gentile world.

What about Orpah? Like many today, she couldn't bring herself to leave the comforts of her old life, her old self and take that step of faith into a new life.

To glean in that day would be a form of panhandling today. Gleaning was indicative of poverty to the extreme. Beloved, <u>before Christ, you and I were in extreme poverty; without hope</u>! Before Boaz, Ruth and Naomi were in extreme poverty and without hope. Do we get the connection? Boaz, whose name means *powerful*, is a non-divine carbon copy of Jesus Christ. Beloved, Boaz saves Ruth and Naomi just as Jesus saves you and me. Boaz is ultimately going to rescue his bride (The Church) in this story (Just looking ahead) from her poverty and in doing so, He rescues Naomi, a Jewess. (Israel)

Time Out: Ruth is a Gentile and Naomi is a Jewess. From Revelation 19:7-9, 21:9 and Revelation 12:1-2 make this connection – Ruth and Naomi are of the feminine gender. The Book of Revelation identifies both Church and Israel in the feminine gender also.

Just how amazing is this Bible? If you are a skeptic, isn't it time to embrace it?

As a man of God, Boaz was obedient to the Law regarding gleaning. He instructed his workers not go back and retrieve a missed sheaf. But he tells them, "If Ruth is following behind you, uh, err, drop a sheaf or two or three if no one is watching." "When (Not if, Ruth is honest, the Church is honest)) she yells at you that you dropped a sheaf, tell her you can't stop for every sheaf that falls behind." "Tell her she can keep it and simply continue on your way."

Now this girl gathered and threshed an ephah of barley which amounted to a bushel.

That would be huge for a one day gathering.

A close examination of verses twenty two and twenty three is more than just a warning to Ruth to exercise here servanthood in the one safe field. It is a warning to us today to remain in the safe fields of Christ and His Church and not cross over into the fields of the endless number of Cults where danger to Salvation lurks.

Additional Insight to Old Testament Law

1) **Gleaning** - Leviticus 19:9-10

Concerns taking care of the poor. This was not to be an entitlement hand out as we see today where it is too often used as a trade-off for pork-barrel political favors. God's Law required work on the part of individuals receiving freebies. Hello!

2) **Caretaker law/Kinsman-Redeemer** – Deuteronomy 25:5

Concerns taking care of family members of deceased blood relatives.

Application

Take rest in this verse: *"May you be richly rewarded by the Lord, the God of Israel, under whose wings you have come to take refuge."* (Ruth 2:12)

Notes for Ruth 2

Ruth 3
Love in Action

"You have not run after men, rich or poor. And now, my daughter, don't be afraid. I will do for you all you ask." (Ruth 3:10) This chapter continues with prophetic overtones. It is at the threshing floor where useful grain to make bread for feeding God's people is separated from useless chaff. The one attending to that purpose here is Boaz. The one seeking his provision is Ruth, which ultimately benefits Naomi.

Theologian Warren Wiersbe offers a worthy outline in reading this chapter. Ruth hears instruction, (vv. 1-4) obeys, (vv. 5-9) believes the word of her redeemer, (vv. 10-14) receives his gifts, (vv. 15-17) then patiently waits for her redeemer to attend the details.

Read Ruth 3:1-9

1) What comes to Naomi's mind that needs to be done regarding Ruth? (v. 1)

2) What important observation about Boaz does Naomi relate to Ruth? (v. 2)

3) What instructions does Naomi give Ruth regarding being presentable to live in the permanent home of a kinsman-redeemer? (vv. 3-4)

4) How well does Ruth receive and respond to Naomi's instructions? (vv. 5-8)

5) When people dismiss wise instruction, what is their central problem? What will be the result when they follow after their own way? See Proverbs 16:18

Discussion:

What do you observe about people who hear the message of Christ but who have discovered what is to them *a better way* that the rest of us haven't discovered?

6) What does Ruth ask of Boaz and on what basis does she make her request? (v. 9) See Ezekiel 16:8

Read Ruth 3:10-18

7) Now Ruth has come to Boaz in needful humbleness. Compare Boaz's reply (v. 11) to John 6:35-37.

8) Recall a time (Maybe too long to remember) you met someone in whom you were more than just casually interested that you desired to develop a close relationship with. Didn't you kind of like, do the leg work to check them out to see if you might stand a chance? What would you say Boaz had already done regarding Ruth and what does that indicate? (v. 12)

9) Name two reasons why a relationship with Ruth might not work out for Boaz?

Note: Ruth laying at the feet of Boaz is the equivalent of knowing that at the feet of Jesus, we have nothing to fear. See Luke 10:39

10) What message does John 19:28-30 bring to you?

11) What does verse fifteen suggest about this man Boaz?

Summary Statement:

This chapter displays Ruth hearing instructions and her response. She doesn't interject additional requirements of herself that in her eyes makes her more attractive to Boaz. <u>A lesson for those who champion church rituals or practice legalism.</u> Further, the chapter highlights the work and benefits of a deliverer.

Question: Have you fully placed your trust in Christ alone, free of mandated edicts?

Verse ten is a noteworthy verse of this chapter and of this small Book of Ruth. Peeling back layers of this verse reveals a description of Ruth and of God's people.

"You have not run after younger men." (Ruth 3:10)

Ruth, our <u>bride</u> to be (God's people, the Church) <u>has not ran after the world</u>. Doesn't mean sin isn't present in her life. (Christ died for sin) It means God's people do not run after the seemingly more attractive things of this world. Things the eyes see and lust after. The *true* Church is not lustful or is it worldly. <u>Christ didn't die for worldliness</u>. Christ died to pay our penalty for sin, but not wanton continual sin! Certainly worldliness is sin, but worldliness is more than sin. Worldliness is a form of idol worship for which the cross did not atone for. Beloved, <u>worldliness is placing appetites ahead of God</u>. God is only an afterthought if that much, to the worldly person.

"And now my daughter, don't be afraid." (Ruth 3:11)

Afraid of what? The destroyer for one thing, but principally here, fear of adequacy to God and His people. <u>Boaz (Christ) will do the heavy lifting to make Ruth (us) legitimate.</u> In this instance, Boaz is addressing the fear of Ruth being accepted among the Jews. Remember, she is a Moabite, and Moabites and Ammonites could not enter the congregation of the Lord. (Deuteronomy 23:2-6)

"I will do for you what you ask." (Ruth 3:11)

By having done the heavy lifting, Christ presents us worthy of dwelling with God's family. All we need do is drop to our knees and <u>rest at His feet.</u>

Unlike the valley location of the winepress, the threshing floor was located at a high elevation so as to make use of the wind to blow away the chaff. Now the threshing floor is symbolic of numerous scriptural truths. It was a place for provision where grain was separated from chaff to provide life sustaining bread. Along with the winepress, the threshing floor was a place in worship. (Deuteronomy 16:13) The two were objects of the law. (Deuteronomy 15:12-14) Joseph mourned Jacob's death at a threshing floor. (Genesis 50:10) And certainly, there are instances in the New Testament where <u>winnowing is associated with separating the saved from the lost</u>. (Matthew 3:12)

What the Gentile Ruth gained that day was also gain for the Jewish Naomi. Israel and the Church one day will become one in Christ. Maranatha!

Hold this thought. Ruth's example of being loved by Boaz is assurance that God's love for His chosen people, Israel, also extends to any Gentile who seeks Him!

Application

"His winnowing fork is in his hand, and he will clear his threshing floor, gathering his wheat into the barn and burning up the chaff with unquenchable fire." (Matthew 3:12)

Might we not also winnow the chaff out of our life?

> *"Anyone who listens to the word but does not do what it says*
> *is like a man who looks at his face in the mirror and, after looking at himself,*
> *goes away and immediately forgets what he looks like."*
> **James 1:23**

<u>Boaz does not resemble the man in the above verse</u>. Without hesitation or excuse, Boaz chooses to meet the need requested of him. If we sit at the feet of Christ, without hesitation, He unselfishly meets our need for Salvation.

Blessings Come by Our Choices
Blessings Come by Our Choices
Blessings Come by Our Choices

When faced with a choice, do we make our choice or do we make the <u>right choice</u>? Herein lies the difference <u>between grain and chaff</u>. The sheep and the goats if you will. (Matthew 25:33) For example: You are busy with an I-pad or engaged with watching a favorite TV program when an elderly person calls just to talk. <u>Joyfully meet a need</u>. Lay aside what pleasures you and engage in a meaningful conversation with this person calling you. Beloved, <u>this is Jesus calling</u>! This elderly person is lonely and has chosen you to <u>bless their life</u>. You should feel truly special <u>they thought of you</u>! For a few minutes, you are a kinsman-redeemer. They thought of you because they could <u>be sure of your kindness</u> and genuine interest in them. This is the picture Boaz and Christ portray. They joyfully meet a need. Christ is genuinely interested in others. He proved this in His ministry and miracles. And certainly, He proved this at the Cross.

It doesn't matter that we attend church, teach Sunday school, sing in the choir or don't smoke or drink. These church activities are little more than corban phoniness if we are neglecting aging parents or a friend or neighbor in need!

May God give us an awareness to make the right choice when faced with a decision to give our time when someone seeks us. Each of us are given opportunities to be somebody's kinsman-redeemer.

Ruth 4
Love's Reward

"Here I am! I stand at the door and knock.
If anyone hears my voice and opens the door,
I will come in and eat with him, and he with me."
"He who has an ear, let him hear."
(Revelation 3:20, 22)

Ruth came as a stranger from a lost people living in Moab, a land hostile to God. She finds redemption by way of the land of Israel. Make this connection and connect the dots of how your own redemption came about as you study this chapter.

Read Ruth 4:1-8

1) This kinsman (Perhaps a brother to Elimelech) of Naomi and Ruth made the initial decision to acquire a parcel of land belonging to Elimelech. Certainly he had in mind owning it someday. Why do you think he changes his mind and concedes the land to Boaz?

2) a. By not redeeming Ruth, what might this unnamed relative represent?
      See Romans 3:20

   b. What is the implications of this for Salvation?

3) What are the three significant words of verse six?_____

Time Out: Read Deuteronomy 25:7-10 and compare with Ruth 4:8. There is no spitting in a face here, but what is described is significant. <u>Boaz acts on behalf of both Naomi and Ruth</u>. The land (Israel) will remain with Naomi. (Jewish people) As Naomi is too old to produce heirs, Ruth will become the wife of Boaz. It is to be through her that heirs will come. If you don't already know this, Ruth and Boaz will become great-grandparents of David. Their son Obed, would begat Jesse, who would become the father of David. This genealogy eventually leads to Mary then Jesus Himself. Isn't our God truly amazing?

Read Ruth 4:9-12

4) What do verses nine through twelve attest to the worth and new found wealth of Ruth?

Read Ruth 4:13-22

5) After the marriage of Boaz to Ruth, what benefits would fall upon Naomi through the birth of this male child? (vv. 14-15)

6) What is the key word in verse fifteen that we could relate to Christ? _____

7) What is the worth of Ruth to Naomi? (v. 15b)

8) What name is given to the baby born to Ruth and Boaz? _____

9) Who would this infant male child one day become the father of? _____

10) What famous future king of Israel would come from Jesse? _____

11) In wrapping of your study of Ruth, what do the following words mean to you?

    a. Faithfulness:

    b. Kindness:

    c. Kinsman:

    d. Redeemer:

    e. Sustainer:

12) Compare verses seventeen through twenty-two with Matthew 1:1-17.

Summary Statement:

This chapter concludes God's preview of the coming of Jesus and the benefits He brings to those who make the decision of Ruth over the decision of Orpah.

By Law, the unnamed relative was first in line to rescue Naomi and Ruth. But he is unable to deliver a sanctuary for the two women. But Boaz is up to the task to take both under his tent. For you and me, the unnamed relative is the Law and Boaz is the Christ. What the Law doesn't accomplish for the Church and Israel, Jesus did!

Ruth offers four <u>actions of love</u>: Love's *decision, faithfulness, kindness and reward*. <u>Hope</u> was surely present in our three principal individuals when they made decisions. Less obvious, but by no means absent, is the Providence of God.

This may be difficult or perhaps even offensive for some, but it was a blessing for Naomi to lose a faithless husband! Elimelech's death was not happen-chance. Think about it, <u>Elimelech was a stumbling-block</u> to his wife Naomi and their two sons. He was more interested in pursuing worldly needs in Moab than praying for famine relief. The Scriptures tell us Moab was detestable in God's sight. So Elimelech was certainly out of the will of God. <u>His decision separated the whole family from God.</u>

Time Out: God was not available at any time or any place in the Old Testament. The giving of the Holy Spirit wouldn't take place for over a millennium. (Acts 2:1-4)

God's Providence is at times a mystery. In Ruth however, it is evident God had a plan and <u>Elimelech was a stumbling block</u>. Being out of the will of God is fraught with peril when it impedes God's purpose for other individuals.

The example of Saul and David is a classic example that not all relationships should be sustained. Certainly toxic ones like this one shouldn't. Had Saul and David kissed and made up, we would not have the Psalms of David. Had Moses and Pharaoh reached some accord concerning straw, you and I would remain lost. <u>In whatever manner a marriage or friendship fails, we cannot rule out God's Providence</u>.

Each of us should examine our own relationships and in wisdom, determine if we are in some way a stumbling-block for someone close to us. If we are, let us have the wisdom to be an asset and not a liability.

How truly magnificent is this book we call the Bible! The concluding verses of Ruth and the beginning verses of Matthew are among numerous examples that Jesus is who

He said He was! *"I and the Father are one."* (John 10:30) *"I am the resurrection and the life. He who believes in me will live, even though he dies; and whoever lives and believes in me will never die."* (John 11:25-26) Do you believe this?" _____

Beloved, if you are not saved, allow the Spirit to deliver you to believe:
Jesus is the Christ.
    God took on the form of a man in the person of Jesus.
        Jesus came to earth to redeem sinners.
            Jesus was crucified unto death by unregenerate men.
                Jesus defeated the grave by raising unto eternal life on the third day.
                    All who receive Jesus as Savior-Redeemer also possess that which He has.
Receive Him now... ... ...

Pray this prayer: "Lord Jesus, I place my trust in You and You alone. I have nothing to offer except myself and my thankfulness. Thank you for taking away my sins. In Jesus's treasured name, Amen."

Application

Keeping the totality of all four chapters, we can only wonder how Orpah ended up! For we surely know her end was not the same as that of Ruth. <u>The rewards for faithfulness far outweigh the discomforts of the deserts should we have to cross one.</u>

This writer has crossed one.

<u>Once Ruth belonged to Boaz, everything belonging to him belonged to her also.</u>

"I go and prepare a place for you.
I will come again and receive you unto myself;
that where I am, there you may be also."
(John 14:3)

Notes for Ruth 4

In question six, you should have entered "sustain" as the key word of verse fifteen.

Christ is the sustainer for the Christian believer throughout all the days of his or her life.

By all <u>legal accounts</u>, Obed is a grandson to Naomi even though there is no blood relationship.

Seven Lessons
The Book of

Esther

Setting the Stage for Esther

The opening verses of Esther reveal the base nature of man. This is why the Apostle Paul calls for you and me to put off the old nature and put on a new nature. *"Those controlled by the sinful nature cannot please God."* (Romans 8:8) You will discover, the Persians in our story of Esther are indeed, a sorry lot. They have no good in them!

Our leading Hebrews, Esther and Mordecai, are what we would call good people. But we shall see they are not godly people. Understand, God had made a way for Hebrews to return to Jerusalem from Babylon and Persia. Those who did not were out of the will of God. Fortunately, Divine Providence saves them from extinction.

How does that translate for us? When we slip away from God's will, God does not abandon us. On that we can rest. God has His own tethered to the Cross. The only subject we can find glorified in Esther is Divine Providence.

God uses people who are not passive when action is required. Just as Rahab became involved, so also did Esther and Mordecai. Had action not been taken, many Hebrews would have been murdered by evil men.

Many believe they can work things out without God. The Book of Esther refutes that way of thinking. Without God's intervention, the only thing we would work out is our own destruction. As Esther unfolds, look for the keeping power of God; His Providence and His Sovereignty. *The Perfect Wisdom of Our God* is an Anthem by Keith Getty/Stuart Townsend that could appropriately accompany the Esther story.

> The perfect wisdom of our God revealed in all the universe.
> All things created by His hand and held together by His command.
> He knows the mysteries of the seas; the secrets of the stars are His.
> He guides the planets on their way and turns the earth through another day.
>
> The perfect timing of His ways along the path of righteousness.
> His word a lamp unto my feet; His Spirit teaching and guiding me.
> And O the wisdom of the cross to save the helpless and the lost.
> He chose the fool to shame the wise that all the glory might go to Christ.
>
> Oh grant me wisdom from above to pray for peace and cling to love.
> And teach me humbly to receive the sun and rain of Your Sovereignty.
> Each strand of sorrow has a place within this tapestry of grace.
> So through the trials I'll choose to say; "Your perfect will in your perfect way."

Esther 1
A Crisis of Insubordination

Set in post Babylon Persia, these Medo-Persian people are governing over the Hebrews who did not return to Jerusalem. Our story opens with the Persian King Xerxes about the business of making a big splash on the world stage of his kingdom. He throws a kingdom wide spectacle for six months climaxing in a weeklong binge drinking event. When he sends for Queen Vashti to join him for the closing festivities, she refuses to participate. Her un-cooperation precipitates a royal crises that is an embarrassment to King Xerxes. The queen's refusal to attend as we shall see, is no accident.

Read Esther 1:1-18

1) What significant information are we given to have us understand the extent King Xerxes went to extol the magnificence of his monarchy? (v. 4)

2) In a word, how might we describe the personality of King Xerxes? _____

3) What weeklong event was to draw to a close this half-year event?

4) What indicates that the concluding banquet was gender divided? (v. 9)

Time Out: Certainly the nobles and the general population had been accompanied by their wives for the king's extravaganza. But the fact that women were separate from the men suggests this was still a business gathering. History tells us this was King Xerxes being about the business of selling himself as being worthy to support for additional military conquests to the west. Specifically, Greece in the immediate future.

5) What was King Xerxes' plan to bring the festivities to a glorious conclusion?

6) When asked to come to the side of her husband, what was Queen Vashti response?

7) What precedent was anticipated to be set by Queen Vashti's refusal to come to the King's side? (vv. 17-18)

Discussion:
We are not told why the queen refused to appear when called by the king. Do you think her choice was wise and why?

8) Who do you think is behind Queen Vashti's decision to not go to her husband?

Read Esther 1:19-22
9) What decree was issued concerning Queen Vashti? (v. 19)

10) What were the implications of the decree against Queen Vashti going to have throughout the empire? (v. 20)

11) What was the final dispatch sent out to all corners of the empire? (v. 22)

12) How does the final dispatch reveal just how really large and vast this empire was?

Summary Statement:
Seemingly, God is absent from this story. But as this story begins to unfold, we will come to understand that God was present from the very first chapter. We have here a Persian king intent on making a big splash of his magnificence all the while his queen wants no part of it. What starts out as a major extravaganza for a king ends in a resounding dud for him.

Author's Note: From watching the TV Drama "House of Cards" starring Kevin Spacey, you can picture the unfolding story in Esther 1. They are in many respects the same.

Historically, Esther is post Babylonian Exile, Nebuchadnezzar and Daniel. The story takes place in relation to the <u>chest and arms of silver</u> part of the statue visions of Daniel 2. The Medo-Persian Empire has replaced the former Babylonian rule. (Circa 539-331 B.C.) Cyrus the great had issued the proclamation for the Jews to return to Jerusalem and rebuild the city and the Temple. Cyrus even decreed the return of the sacred vessels of worship to go with the returning Hebrews. But not all the Jews returned to Jerusalem. Fewer than sixty thousand is said to have returned. <u>These are the Hebrews in God's will</u>. For they were the work force from which Nehemiah would draw from to restore Jerusalem. The greater number of Hebrews who remained in Exile were too comfortable to pull up stakes and move across the desert.

Esther unfolds an account of the survival of the Hebrews who remained in a pagan land. Their zeal for God once demonstrated by Daniel and his three friends has been lost. Though the Hebrews here are out of God's will, <u>they are not out of His sight</u>. Esther is the only account of these people. Out of these unreturning Hebrews, no progress would result that would point toward anything relating to the Christ. As a result, no passage from the Book of Esther is ever quoted in the New Testament.

Note: Take time to examine the Song of Deborah in Judges, Chapter 5. The Hebrews had just experienced victory over an arch enemy. Go through the song and circle the number of times Deborah gives reference to the Lord. The story of Esther closes with an account of their triumph over their enemies. Sadly, there is no song of Esther or any praise of God.

Because God knows evil is brewing for His people, He sets about the business of changing the dynamics even in this pagan empire. Whatever we might conclude about queen Vashti, we can be sure she is in no position to circumvent the evil that is just around the corner for God's people. For this reason, just as God moved Pharaoh to reach the decisions he reached, we can be sure God is behind Queen Vashti's decision to not appear at the king's grand climax.

King Xerxes is your typical pagan ruler that appears throughout history. Many remain on the scene today. They abhor disappointment. The queen is set aside and her replacement is on the horizon. For her, it was obviously not a wise decision. But for God's people, it couldn't have been better.

Application

"We know that in all things God works for the good of those who love him, who have been called according to his purpose. For those God foreknew he also predestined to be conformed to the likeness of his Son, that he might be the firstborn among many brothers. And those he predestined, he also called; those he called, he also justified; those he justified, he also glorified." (Romans 8:28-30)

Notes for Esther 1

Esther 2
Finding a New Queen

It goes without saying, Persian kings accumulated many women. In charge of the women as always, were emasculated male eunuchs. In this chapter, we meet our first principal Jew, Mordecai, from the Tribe of Benjamin. We also meet Hadassah otherwise known as Esther. Esther is Mordecai's young cousin. She has been adopted by Mordecai after the young girl's parents had died.

The action that unfolds is precipitated by King Xerxes and his ongoing efforts to find himself a new queen. Along the way, a plot to dispose the king is uncovered.

Read Esther 2:1-18

1) How old would Mordecai have been when he went into exile into Babylon?

2) Regarding Esther's nationality, what had been Mordecai's instruction to her?

3) Of the many girls that were brought into the king's court at the Citadel of Susa, how did Esther fare in relation to the many other young women assembled?

4) How long was the preparation period for these anticipated young women? (v. 12)

Discussion:

Do you think these young maidens considered themselves abused or do think they felt honored? What would be the reaction of today's western woman in similar circumstances?

5) What was King Xerxes's assessment of Esther and what was the end result?

Read Esther 2:19-23

6) What secret about herself did Esther continue in maintaining?

Discussion:

Without knowing the rest of the story, what might you be thinking about Esther's mindset regarding her secret that she was a Jew?

7) Where did Mordecai eventually come to be located in the king's court?

8) From his position, what secret did Mordecai come to find out?

9) To whom did Esther give credit for information discovered about the plot to assassinate the king?

10) What was the action that followed the discovery of the plot to assassinate the king?

11) Regarding Mordecai, what is missing at the close of this chapter that you would expect to occur?

Time Out: Not much has changed in the world. Covetousness for power is an ever present danger for many heads of state in the world. Until Jesus returns and assumes control, history will continue to repeat itself regarding plots to overthrow leaders.

Summary Statement:

Without a queen to confide his thoughts, King Xerxes' attendants propose searching for a new queen. Young virgins are gathered to be prepped in a year long process. A new player is introduced in the person of Mordecai, a Hebrew. Mordecai proves to be invaluable to King Xerxes in two ways. Mordecai saves the king's life and provides the king a worthy candidate to be queen.

To better understand the mood of Xerxes to begin this chapter, we have to turn to the New King James Version. *"After these events."* (Esther 1:1 NKJV) After what events? The Bible doesn't tell us but world history does. Xerxes followed up on his preparation to expand his empire to the west and begin to chip away at the Greek Empire. But his Persian army was no match for the fighting prowess of the Greeks. Daniel's vision of the Medo-Persian Empire giving way to the Greek Empire (Daniel 2:32) was already being put into God's progressive plan for men and nations.

Resoundingly turned back by the Greeks, Xerxes is now back in his palace in Susa. With Queen Vashti now deposed, he has no one to confide in. Moreover, the decree to dispose her could not be overturned even by a king.

Finding her replacement now goes forward in full swing. Even though God is never mentioned, we can be certain <u>He is near and actively involved</u>.

Nothing to this point in Esther suggests anything having to do with the things of God. Our first indication of anything thing having to do with God is the Jew <u>Mordecai, from the Tribe of Benjamin</u>. (Keep Mordecai's tribal membership in mind for later insight.) Mordecai was one of many Hebrews who had decided not to return to his own land with his people.

Think about it, Joseph served God's purpose in Egypt and Daniel served God's purpose in Babylon. <u>Service to God can occur anywhere God has a purpose</u>. Unlike the stories of Rahab and others, Mordecai and Esther appear as poor examples of people of Faith as we understand them. Yet, <u>people can still remain in the Providence and purpose of God</u>. Keep this thought, the Jews are still a captive people and anti-Semitism has not abated.

Recall the diets of Daniel and his three friends were thought to be less than adequate to compete, yet they excelled. (Daniel 1) The same is true here regarding beauty treatments. Esther's beauty exceeded those of her rivals. When she went before the king, she was chancing being placed in the commune of concubines. But by the Providence of God, <u>Esther is selected to be the new queen</u>.

In addition to Esther's crowning beauty, with information given her by Mordecai, she is <u>instrumental in saving the king from a plot to kill him</u>. There is no indication at this point in the narrative of any reward for Mordecai's service.

Application

A beauty pageant and an assassination plot both fall under the Providence of God. For those who belong to God, no event is outside His will for the good of those who love the Lord.

"We speak the wisdom of God in a mystery, the hidden wisdom which God ordained before the ages for our glory." "Eye has not seen, nor ear heard, nor have entered into the heart of man the things which God has prepared for those who love Him.
(1 Corinthians 2:7-9 NKJV)

Our God is truly amazing in how He watches over us. Rejoice in that thought!

Notes for Esther 2

Esther 3
An Evil Man can only do Evil

Our bad guy Haman is an Agagite. (v. 1) Agagites were the royal line of Amalekites. These people were the seed of the anti-Semitism we see in the world today. To better understand the events going forward, this lesson will briefly revisit the account of the time God instructed King Saul to destroy to the last man, woman and child the Amalekite society. King Saul's neglect in this matter centuries earlier sets up a potential disaster for the Hebrew people in the Medo-Persian Period. Where Saul failed, the Providence of God is now needed to insure the survival of those Jews who hadn't returned to Jerusalem.

Read Deuteronomy 25:17-19 and 1 Samuel 15:1-3, 7-11, 18-19

1) What was the track record of the Amalekites toward the Hebrew people?

2) What were the armies of the Hebrews instructed to do regarding the Amalekites?

3) What is the message of 1 Samuel 15:22?

4) What was God's reaction to King Saul's disobedience? (1 Samuel 15:23)

Author's Note: Four years have gone by since Esther was installed as queen. In that time Haman, an aristocratic nobleman whose ancestry connects him to being a descendent of the royal order of Amalekites, has been given a high governmental position. The Amalekites hated the Hebrews and had attempted to exterminate them during the desert wanderings. (Exodus 17:8-16)

Read Esther 3:1-7

5) What was it that Mordecai refused to do that would identify him with God? (v. 2)

6) What was the emotional reaction of Haman when he discovered that Mordecai would not bow down in his presence?

7) When Haman found out that Mordecai was a Jew, what far reaching action beyond killing Mordecai was he determined to do? (v. 6)

Discussion:
A game of spin the bottle (Casting lots) would determine the date the extermination of Jews would begin. Verse seven tells us the extermination wouldn't begin for nearly a year. What leads you to consider God had a hand in this little game of darts?

Read Esther 3:8-15
8) What is it that Haman relates to King Xerxes? What is Haman's suggestion about the situation? (vv. 8-9)

9) Money talks. What does Haman tell the king he will do for the soldiers who are given the task of exterminating the Jews?

10) What might indicate that the king couldn't care less about the lives of the Jews living throughout the empire? (v. 11)

11) Describe the preparations that were made to exterminate all Jews.

12) What does verse fifteen reveal about the general public's thoughts of the king's edict to kill an entire ethnic group of people?

Discussion:
In the last one hundred years, who issued similar edicts against the Jews for their extermination? How well did that end for the person issuing anti-Semitic decrees?

Summary Statement:
The Jewish people of this time had committed no crimes, yet they are marked for punishment by extermination. This is an example that when evil is in power, no good can ever come from it without Divine intervention.

Other than inside Israel, no Jew is truly free from ethnic scorn in any part of the world today! Amazingly, there are and have always been anti-Semitic individuals even in our churches who claim to follow Christ but are seemingly oblivious that Jesus was a Jew.

Hatred for the Jewish people has been with us since before the Exodus. This is how dense the mind of a Jew hater is. <u>The Jew has survived the worst the world has hurled against them!</u> Still, Jewish enemies persist. The likes of Pharaoh, Adolph Hitler, Antiochus Epiphanes and our fellow Haman in this chapter are all in the ground awaiting Judgment. (Revelation 20:11-15) The earth belongs to God (Exodus 19:5) and God has chosen out of the earth the Jew as His Covenant People.

> *"For you are a holy people to the Lord your God,*
> *and the Lord has chosen you to be a people for Himself,*
> *a special treasure above all the peoples*
> *who are on the face of the earth."*
> **Deuteronomy 14:2**

<u>Nations who desire to destroy Israel are already under Judgment</u> and we see evidence of that today in the suffering of anti-Semitic societies. Beloved, if you have distaste for the Jewish people or any ethnicity for that matter, ask Jesus to lift that burden from your heart. <u>Extermination of the Jews is just not going to happen</u>. The only city on earth that survives to the end of the Book of Revelation is Jerusalem! Maranatha!

Though we don't get a testimony about God from Mordecai, his actions speak his mind and his heart. He is not one to bow to a mortal man. The decree that goes out to kill all Jews is even puzzling to all the ethnic groups of the Persian Empire. The Jews are living in peace and have done nothing to deserve such horrific punishment.

Most of us can shrug off an insult, but prideful bullies will seek revenge when slighted. Haman was such a person. Literature, apart from Scripture, tells us it was not unusual for nobles of that day to order lashes even for inanimate objects when the objects didn't do their bidding. There is a story that Xerxes ordered lashes for a water spring when it wouldn't do what he told it to do.

"The Lord examines the righteous,
but the wicked and those who love violence his soul hates.
Psalm 11:5

There is a bit of irony in this chapter. Mordecai a Benjamite, is the catalyst to bring down a descendant of the royal order of the Amalekite aristocracy. This man Haman is alive as a result of another Benjamite named Saul. When Saul was king over Israel, he was told to completely take out the Amalekites because they harbored such hatred for the Hebrews. Not only did King Saul not carry out that order, he allowed his army to take forbidden plunder.

Application

All who trifle with God's people will ultimately experience His Wrath! There is a supernatural reason for anti-Semitism. He is called the devil. (1 Peter 5:8)

"A great and wondrous sign appeared in heaven: a woman clothed with the sun, the moon under her feet and a crown of twelve stars on her head. She was pregnant and cried out in pain as she was about to give birth. Then another sign appeared in heaven; an enormous red dragon with seven heads and ten horns and seven crowns on his heads. His tail swept a third of the stars out of the sky and flung them to the earth. The dragon stood in front of the woman who was about to give birth, so that he might devour her child the moment it was born. She gave birth to a son, a male child, who will rule all the nations." **Revelation 12:1-5**

Fortunately for the Church, Jesus came through the Jew to thwart the devil's plans.

Notes for Esther 3

Esther 4
Ritual in place of Intimacy

If you have some Bible study under your belt, you will quickly sense there is something missing in this chapter. Where is prayer? Not one is crying out to God for deliverance.

Evil has stuck its ugly head up and the Hebrew people are aware they are in great danger of being murdered by the tens of thousands. But <u>religious ritual of sack cloth and ashes</u> is substituted for cries for mercy. We can safely say they believe in God, but they are oblivious to the need to turn to Him in a crisis situation.

Suffice to say, the same situation exist today. There are far more believers than there are prayer warriors.

Read Esther 4:1-8

1) We have learned in earlier chapters that when a law was made and sealed by the king, even he couldn't undo the law.

   a. If you had the power, what law would you make that would be unalterable?

   Explain:

   b. Is there a present law you would permanently set aside today? Explain:

2) Compare Mordecai's actions (v. 1) with Daniel's action in Daniel 9:3-11, 17-18.

3) What was Queen Esther's response to Mordecai making a spectacle of himself throughout the city of Susa? (v. 4)

4) What was it that Hannah did that Esther did not do? See 1 Samuel 2:1-10

5) To understand what was troubling Mordecai to be making such a spectacle of himself within the city, Esther sent a messenger to gain additional information. What did Mordecai tell Esther's messenger concerning the Jews? (v. 8)

6) What was it that Mordecai wanted Esther to do on behalf of all Jews?

Read Esther 4:9-17

7) How many days had passed that the king had not summoned the queen to come to him? What might be the implications of the king not wanting to see the queen for such an extended period?

8) Upon Mordecai receiving the information of Esther's absence from the king, what did he want her to understand about herself? (v. 13)

9) Even though Mordecai has yet to pray, we still get a picture of his mind in verse fourteen. What do you think Mordecai is aware of in verse fourteen?

10) What is your assessment of this part of verse fourteen? *"And who knows but that you have come to royal position for such a time as this."*

11) At risk to her own life, Esther makes plans to go to the king on behalf of all Jews. What might her requests (v. 16) suggest about her belief concerning Yahweh? See also Joshua 6:2-5 and 2 Kings 5:14

12) In all of this, what is noticeably absent from the actions of both Esther and Mordecai? See Joshua 5:14 and Revelation 1:17

Summary Statement:

The Jews are in danger of genocide. Still, we can be sure that such will not happen. Verse fourteen sums up this chapter with this profound statement; *"For if you remain silent at this time, relief and deliverance for the Jews will arise from another place, but you and your father's family will perish."* (Esther 4:14)

As previously stated, <u>the Hebrews who did not return to Jerusalem were living out of the will of God</u>. When people live out of the will of God you can be sure their prayer life is nonexistent. Where prayer is absent, intimacy with the Lord is just not possible. From question two, an examination of Daniel 9 revealed Daniel, unlike Mordecai, was to the core of his being, intimately connected with the Lord.

This chapter quickly reveals that Mordecai, to his credit, is a believer by the fact that he tore his clothes and put on sackcloth and ashes. This custom was a traditional ritual of believing Jews. It is much the same as our public water baptism in New Testament times. <u>Both are an outward sign of an internal condition</u>. What is troubling however; considering tens of thousands of Jews are in harm's way of being murdered, the principals of our story, Mordecai and Esther, do not go to Yahweh in prayer. Belief is obviously there, but intimacy was absent. We observe this today. There are many believers, but prayer warriors are few.

- J. Vernon McGee identifies the reason for a lack of prayer is the absence of conviction for sin. The Church, he says, is responsible for it. Sin is just not a popular subject. Conviction for sin is foreign to the hearts and lives of unbelievers and it doesn't set well with believers. The average believer says "I trust Christ," but he has no real conviction of sin in his life at all. Sin is absent in contemporary Church life. <u>When is the last time you heard someone cry for mercy</u>?

To answer McGee's question "when is the last time you heard someone cry for mercy," it is probably Daniel! In our story here, no one takes it upon themselves to pray. When people are out of the will of God, prayer is not on their agenda. When Jonah was running from God, prayer was the last thing on his mind. (Jonah 1:1-3) Fortunately for all of us, when we are out of the will of God, Our Lord loves us enough to move in providential ways to our benefit and to His glory.

This author speaks with firsthand knowledge of this fact. If you give it some thought, you who are reading this can say much the same thing about yourself. Jonah shouldn't have been on that boat! Even so, God took care of Jonah in perhaps a less than pleasant way. <u>There are consequences when we are out of God's will</u>.

We should note, in verse fourteen, Mordecai speaks with the authority of a Prophet.

We also see a similarity between Esther's words in verse sixteen and the words of Shadrach, Meshach and Abednego in Daniel 3:17-18.

In conclusion, Ester's decision to go before the king when not summoned by him was a brave act on the order of Rahab. (Joshua 2:1-6) Another person who put Himself in harm's way was Jesus coming down to earth and positioning Himself among the most dangerous of all creatures, mortal man.

Application

When evil is at work in the world or even in your life, what are you doing about it?

Let's hope we do what Daniel did, <u>go to the Lord in prayer</u>. But even if we don't, our glorious Lord knows what is coming and that is why we can trust Him. Once we put our hand in His hand, we are assured He has the power to deliver us from evil.

- Referenced from Through the Bible Commentary Series J. Vernon McGee Thomas Nelson Copyright 1991 by Thru the Bible Radio. ISBN 0-7852-1016-4 (TR) ISBN 0-7852-1082-2 (NRM) ISBN: 978-0-7852-0427-5

Notes for Esther 4

Esther 5-6
Illusions of an Evil Man

"Do not fret because of evil men or be envious of those who do wrong, for like the grass they will soon wither, like green plants they will soon die away. (Psalm 37:11-2)

Read Esther 5:1-8

1) Describe Esther's appearance when she appeared before King Xerxes. What was his response? (vv. 2-3)

2) What was Esther's request regarding Haman? (v. 4)

3) How many banquets did Esther host for the king and Haman? _____

Discussion:

Why the need for two banquets? Would you wine and dine somebody more than once for a favor? Might there be a biblical message here?

Read Esther 5:9-14

4) On his way home from the palace, what event occurred that further inflamed Haman against Mordecai?

5) What was Haman's response to all of the attention directed his way from Esther and the king?

6) What did Haman's wife and friends suggest to be done about Mordecai?

7) How would you describe both the character of Haman and his mindset about himself?

Discussion:

Is Haman any different from proud unbelievers of today who build their lives on self-adulating illusions? What are some illusions of unbelievers regarding Heaven?

Read Esther 6:1-14

8) What had been overlooked and now was revealed to the king when the chronicles of his reign were read to him during a night of sleeplessness? (vv. 1-3)

9) What was the purpose of Haman's visit to the king? (v. 4)

10) What is the irony of verse six?

Discussion:
Think of a time you thought something bad was going to happen for you but to your surprise good came to you! Has there ever been a time when you imagined good coming your way but you experienced just the opposite?

11) What lessons do we learn here about investing in advanced presumptions?

12) Verses six through nine describes great honor being exhibited by the king towards a yet unnamed individual. Who ultimately receives the king's honor? (v. 10)

13) Compare Haman's demeanor when he returned home for the second time in Esther 6:12 to his first return in Esther 5:9-12. What had changed?

14) What was Haman's fate predicated upon that has ramifications for nations today? (v. 13)

Summary Statement:
Haman represents today's lost. Those living under the illusion; there was no Christ, the resurrection never occurred, God does not exist, Israel is illegitimate, there is no Judgment, neither Heaven nor hell exists. These folks live for the pleasures of now!

"For the message of the cross is foolishness to those who are perishing."
(1 Corinthians 1:18)

Accessing the Scriptures

Is this not surreal? Esther already has a banquet prepared for the king and Haman. (v. 5:4) This is a no-brainer as to who planted this idea on her heart. Further, God knew her mind that <u>she was a risk taker in the manner of Rahab</u>. God knows each of us. If we are a believer willing to roll up our sleeves, He uses us!

Esther basically takes a leap of faith when she breaks a law by appearing before the king without being summoned by him. As she does so, glance back to the previous chapter, verse sixteen. *"And if I perish, I perish."* (Esther 4:16) Has she trusted God? There is no indication she has. Does she pray? No, she does not. Still, she knows her Jewish heritage and God's promises regarding her people. Might she be resting on this hope?

There is no testimony of faith here on the part of anyone. But <u>there is testimony on the Providence of God</u>. Contrary to the law of the land, the king is delighted Esther has come to him. God has used the king's natural nature, vanity, to procure the response needed at this very moment. What happens in these few seconds will determine the triumph of good over evil; life instead of death for tens of thousands of Hebrews. Perhaps a million lives are being saved at this very moment concerning the Jews living in the Persian Empire. It is not a stretch to relate this same triumph the instant Jesus opened his eyes in that tomb. <u>In that instant</u>, reprieve for millions from Judgment and death was accomplished!

> *"Where, O death is your victory? Where, O death, is your sting?"*
> **1 Corinthians 15:55**

Some folks are just inherently evil. Haman is such a person. He, like Antiochus Epiphanes, was a Hitler of this ancient age. Genocide of Jews were a part of their agendas. Haman is best described as a snake that has crawled out of an oil slick. Haman is typical of proud individuals today who live in the world of self-adulation.

Many have risen to dictatorships of their countries. They bask in false confidence living with the illusion they, not God, are the center of the universe. Such folks are totally <u>oblivious the shadow of death is upon them.</u> Their glory is their defeat as is the case with this fellow Haman. To a lesser extent, you may know of such a person. They desperately need prayers. More than likely, no one has ever prayed for them.

Chapters five, six and seven are a prefiguration of the Book of Revelation. In these three chapters we have two feasts. <u>There are two feasts in the Book of Revelation</u>. The attempt by the anti-Semitic Haman to exterminate the Jews is himself extinguished. This attempt is repeated in the Book of Revelation. (Revelation 20:9) The triumph of good over evil taking place in the story of Esther is really refreshing in light of the world today when it seems as though arrogant men, greedy for power and wealth, seem invincible. Their violence is appalling but beloved, their end is already sealed! Maranatha!

Application

If you know a Haman kind of person, they are perhaps that way because, rather than being showered with prayer in their life, they have been showered with worldliness.

If you trust the Bible and all that is in it, you know what awaits them. <u>Pray for them</u>.

Also, it is not a good idea to hate the Jew or to be opposed to the existence of Israel!

Notes for Esther 5-6

Esther 7-8
Evil Defeated, Joy Prevails

The king is informed that his queen, along with her people have been placed under a death sentence. Years earlier a plot to murder the king was exposed. (Esther 2:22) Now there is a plan in place in which the king himself has been duped into signing that would see this queen executed. (Ester 3:10-13) Suffice to say, such skullduggery against the king's household did not set well with King Xerxes. He would have none of it.

Read Esther 7:1-10

1) How long did this second banquet hosted by Esther for the king and Haman last?

2) Esther never went to the Lord in prayer. Do you think two days of wine drinking (if she did) gave her the courage she displays? (vv. 2-4)

3) What secret about herself would Esther be revealing in verses two, three and four?

4) What is revealed to the king about Haman? (vv. 4-6)

5) a. What is the king's reaction concerning what Esther told him? (vv. 5-7)

   b. What is the reaction of Haman when Esther spilled the beans on him?

6) What unflattering position did the king misconstrue about Haman in verse eight?

Author's Note: *"As soon as the words left the king's mouth, servants covered Haman's face."* (Esther 7:8) It was the custom of that time for a king's attendants to sense when the king was so incensed, execution was prepared without the order being formally issued. Haman's head was immediately covered for execution.

7) What was the irony of the gallows on which Haman would be hanged!

Read Esther 8:1-14

8) What are the details of what happens to Haman's Estate?

9) What favor does Esther plead to the king? (8:3-5)

10) What verse fully reveals that Esther is Jewish?

11) Of the new decree that is to be written concerning the Jews, who is given the task to write the decree?

12) Since the old decree called for the Jews to be exterminated, what was the next best thing that could be done to protect the Jews? (v. 11)

Read Esther 8:15-17

13) How would you compare with what was happening to Mordecai in verse fifteen to what was planned to happen to him in Esther 5:14?

14) What is the plan of the devil for the people of the earth? See 1 Peter 5:8

Discussion:

How do you personally compare the end of chapter eight with what you know from the final chapters (Revelation 19 thru 22) of the Book of Revelation?

Summary Statement:

The king in this narrative comes to the aid of those condemned by the devil's agent!

In the economy of God, evil will be exposed as it is here. Evil's glory is its destruction. By God's design, <u>evil in this story even builds its own gallows</u>. To add insult to injury, God stuck His leg out tripping Haman causing him to fall on top of the queen so that he was certain to draw the ire of the king. (At just the right moment)

Let us consider the position of a proud king. He had deposed a queen some years earlier for insubordination. That was no accident. God's hand was in the first queen's decision to be insubordinate. Now the king is faced with the possibility of sending his present queen into slavery or worse, executing her along with a lot of people who had done the king no wrong. Unfortunately for Haman, he is the culprit for placing the king in what was surely an embarrassing predicament. Surely, the devil cringed as he sees his pawn exposed.

One has to wonder how Esther gets up her courage to get around to spilling the beans of her Jewish heritage. Unlike Daniel and others who placed their courage in the Lord, Esther seems to have acquired her courage from two days of drinking. (v. 2)

Since a law that could not be revoked was now enforce to attack and kill Jews, the best thing to defang this law was to issue a new law giving the Jews the right to assemble. We would call this today, armed militias. <u>These Jewish militias were even granted the right to plunder an antagonist's possessions</u>. Which means, the herds the attacker's family depended on for food could be in jeopardy. This new edict would certainly discourage attacking and killing Jews. Suffice to say, just as God used Esther, Mordecai and yes, a pagan king to preserve Israel in that day, God uses America today to preserve the Jewish people. *"Blessed is the nation whose God is the Lord."* (Psalm 33:12) Beloved, may we never forget that!

Chapter 8 is one of the Old Testament's wonderful examples of New Testament Salvation. The Jews living in the Persian Empire were out of the will of God. But by the Grace of God, Divine Providence saved them anyway. You and I have lived out of the will of God. <u>Who can say he is without sin</u>? But beloved, by Divine Grace given us in the person of Christ Jesus, we are saved!

With evil now deposed, <u>the bride of the king benefits from an inheritance.</u> Both the Bride and Mordecai the Jew, come into the presence of the King. (Sound familiar?) For those who have studied the Book of Revelation. you will surely get a prophetic picture of all of this.

The end of chapter eight is one of total victory for the Jews of Susa and Jews everywhere living in the Persian Empire. In fact, this victory was so joyous, non-Jews <u>celebrated with the Jews.</u> What a marvelous foreshadow of the joyous victory that will take place when Christ returns and <u>joins together Israel and the Church.</u> This event is vividly ascribed in The Book of Revelation. Maranatha!

Application

Esther is another certainty that the Jew is God's Covenant People. Haman represents Anti-Semitism of the highest order and is ever present in the world. The question is, is there Anti-Semitism in your heart? How do you feel about the Jew? Beloved, if you harbor even an ounce of resentment for God's people, ask the Spirit to soften you heart and deliver you from such sentiments.

A personal truth here is to understand that perfection you and I cannot offer for our own Salvation. Neither King Xerxes, Esther nor Mordecai can be credited with sparing the Hebrews living in Medo-Persia. <u>It was the hand of God</u>! To God be the glory.

"For it is by grace you have been saved through faith,
and that not of yourselves, it is the gift of God.
Not of works lest anyone should boast."
Ephesians 2:8-9 NKJV

Notes for Esther 7-8

Esther 9-10
Attack, Victory, Celebration

The Bible teaches believers not to expect a payoff in this life but to anticipate rich reward in the world to come. That doesn't mean good things don't happen in this life. Esther is a prime example of a payoff in this life <u>if it serves God' purpose</u>! This is true when Divine Providence takes the form of caring, governing, protecting, sustaining or persevering to exercise God's will through His superintendence.

These final two chapters reveal recipients who never entered into prayer benefiting from a miracle of God for deliverance. God's promise to Abraham, Isaac and Jacob is certainly manifested here. The Jewish people remained under God's tent.

Read Esther 9:1-19

1) When the enemies of the Jews attacked, who was victorious?

2) What was most likely on the minds of those who did not participate in attacking Jewish communities? See Joshua 2:10-11 and 3:15-17

3) What happened to the ten sons of Haman on the first day of fighting?

4) To add insult to injury, what was Esther's request to the king regarding what was to be done on the second day with the dead bodies of Haman's ten sons? (vv. 12-13)

Discussion:

The death toll of Jews killing their enemies had to have been enormous! One would think this carnage and turmoil throughout the provinces would concern the nation's leader. Why does it appear this king seems more concerned with Esther's wishes then he is about the sectarian fighting in the streets of his capital city?

5) a. What occurred on the fourteenth day of the final month (Adar, early spring month) of the Jewish year out in the provinces?

   b. What is different about the celebration of Purim in the capitol city of Susa?

Optional: If someone in your class is familiar with Jewish observances, give them a few minutes to explain them or perhaps, have a prepared handout.

6) a. What is common to verses ten, fifteen and sixteen?

   b. Why do you think the Jews never did take the plunder when they very well could have? See 1 Samuel 15:1-3, 9-19

   c. By not taking the plunder, what might we conclude about these Jews and their mindset about God?

Read Esther 9:20-10:3

7) a. What does Chapter 10 indicate about Mordecai's relationship with the king?

   b. Name two other Jews who were held in high esteem by pagan emperors?
   See Genesis 41:39-40 and Daniel 2:48

8) What was Esther's official action that confirmed Mordecai's communication to all the Jewish people in the empire? (vv. 29, 32)

Discussion:
Relating Chapter 10 to today, do you know of Christians successfully serving non-Christians? Why do you think unbelievers place trust in believers?

Summary Statement:
Esther ends really well for the Jews. So much so that the celebration of Purim, though not Mosaic, is observed in Jewish society around the world today.

"Then Noah built an altar to the Lord." (Genesis 8:20) *"There Abraham built an altar to the Lord and called on the name of the Lord."* (Genesis 12:8) *"So Gideon built an altar to the Lord."* (Judges 6:24) We can recite other additional examples of individuals constructing altars to the Lord but you get the picture. Our two principle characters and their people in this entire story are Jewish. But awareness of God is not apparent other than, plunder is never taken following victories over their enemies.

You and I don't have to construct an altar to the Lord, because if we have been regenerated, the Holy Spirit has already built His Temple in us. (1 Corinthians 6:16) God can be found wherever we go. We may have a special place in the home to read the Bible and pray, but even when we are away from home, God is still with us. (Deuteronomy 31:8, Hebrews 13:5)

None of the Jews in our story are recorded taking material goodies from their victories even though the king did allow it! In Christ, we have attained victory over the world. Therefore, forbid us to not take from the world the plunder it offers; worldliness, covetousness, lust, licentiousness and what the flesh desires. Plunder is dangerous because it can replace the Lord as first in our lives. See Revelation 2:4-5

How we spend our leisure time speaks as much about us as the booty we acquire. Would Jesus enter a bar? Certainly, but with the purpose of 1 Peter 3:19. Would Jesus enter a department store? Certainly, but it would not be His natural habitat. Beloved, we speak of worldliness, not sin. Know the difference! Christ died for your sins because God loves you. Christ didn't die so you could love the world. Worldliness means to love the Creation more than the Creator! We cannot love both God and the world. *"Seek first the kingdom of heaven."* (Matthew 6:24) Suffice to say, there is more attention to texting than to widows and orphans in this generation!

The hanging of Haman's ten sons on the second day (vv. 13-14) is after the fact of their having been killed on the first day. (vv. 6-7) Severe it will be for nations or individuals who scorn the Jews. No amount of church attendance or reverence for some semblance of a heavenly God will set aside anti-Semitism. (Genesis 12:3, Jeremiah 30:16-17)

Time Out: Now there are some folks that hold the Jews responsible for various ills of society as well as the execution of Jesus. For these and other reasons, these folks are just anti-Semitic. In short, like

Haman, they are of the devil. Scripture is clear, if you dislike a Jewish person, or anyone for that matter, don't let it be for ethnic reasons.

Application

"God did not reject his people, whom he foreknew"
Romans 11:2

Had Haman been privy to the above statement of the Apostle Paul, perhaps he would have not been so adamant on viewing the Jewish people as unworthy of living. There are sects today who have access to Paul's statement in the Bible but still, they harbor disdain for the Jew and others not of their skin. Let no one who calls himself a Christian reject the Jewish people. Christ was a Jew.

These final two chapters reveal <u>a God in control of men, government and nations</u>. To put this in a modern perspective, if your man is not in the white house, don't get all worked up! <u>God's man is in the white house</u>! He may be godly or absolutely pagan. None the less, <u>he is God's man to orchestrate a purpose</u>. Don't let the media work your mind into a frenzy of suspicion and fear. (Psalm 56:3, John 14:27, 2 Timothy 1:7) Such journalism is of the devil. Instead, do your part and vote. <u>Then rest on God</u>. He is in control. Beloved, after an election, (even if you lose) sleep well knowing God's program is on schedule.

Notes for Esther 9-10

Thirteen Lessons
The Epistle to the

Romans

MY
Knees
Give Way

For
He Is Holy

About Romans

Romans is the flagship of Christian Doctrine (Chapters 1-8) and Christian living. (Chapters 12-16) In between these two sections, the Apostle (One who is sent) gives a historical perspective. (Chapters 9-11) Because Chapter 8 segues so well into Chapter 12, this is the order presented in this study. You may follow your Bible's order if you choose.

Being the first letter in our Bible, it may appear the Apostle wrote it first. That is not the case. Roman's is placed first in the Bible because of its importance. In it, the Apostle addresses the righteousness of God and the depravity of men. This is not a message the world wants to hear. To the contrary, the world is in love with the glory of mankind, its successes and technological advances. The concept of living by Faith as addressed in Romans, is objectionable to our works-minded culture. Being God's choice, Paul is the catalyst to bring to repentance (Changed mind) anyone who will listen.

Romans offers a few challenges as you will discover. The concept that some are predestined to be lost while others are elected to be saved should not be allowed to just slide by. (8:28-30) Sovereignty is another challenge. (9:6-29) For example, is God in charge of the occupant in the oval office or is it the electorate? Which brings us to Romans 13:1-7. Are we to honor the nation's leader if we didn't vote for him? Should we rebel against government if its ways are not our ways or even God's way?

This Church in Rome (Not Roman Catholic) was established by some of the individuals identified in the final chapter and not Paul himself. We must assume these folks were among Paul's converts. We could easily say Paul established this Church in absentia. The letter was written while Paul was at Corinth during his third missionary journey.

As you read and study Romans, imagine yourself living in first century Rome and ignorant in matters of religious knowledge. Certainly you wouldn't know anything about Israel. More than likely, your only experience with worship and religion centered on the Emperor and a few silly statues. The author is aware of this and so he presents his case for Christ with the polish of a Divine Herald.

If you are new to Bible study, Paul was the chief spokesperson for the Gospel (Good news) of Jesus Christ. He authored thirteen letters of the New Testament. An account of his conversion is found in the Book of Acts, chapters nine and twenty-two. Paul's letter to the Romans should be read intently and with prayerful deliberation.

Romans 1
Testimony – Revelation – Foolishness

Not yet having visited Rome, Paul's letter will be read mostly to people he had never met. Before one man will listen to another, credibility must first be established. Paul sets out immediately to qualify himself in verse one. After that, the focus of the letter is on revelation, thankfulness for other believers and the foolishness of men.

Read Romans 1:1-7

1) From the following three truths, circle which is the greater for you?

    a. *"Paul, a servant of Christ Jesus, called to be an Apostle."* (Romans 1:1)

    b. *"we receive grace."* (Romans 1:5)

    c. *"was declared with power to be the Son of God by His resurrection."*
    (Romans 1:4)

Explain your choice:

2)   a. Who is the *we* Paul alludes to in verse five?

    b. Who might also the *we* imply?

3) Using a Bible dictionary, circle the word that best describes *set apart.* (v. 1)

Justified – Sanctified – Glorified

Read Romans 1:8-17

4) What is the power Paul speaks of in verse sixteen? (v. 16) See Romans 1:4

5) Of the following truths of this section, which best attracts you to other believers?

    a. *"because their faith is reported all over the world."* (Romans 1:8)

    b. *"I may impart to them some spiritual gift."* (Romans 1:11)

    c. *"that you and I may be mutually encouraged by each other's faith."*
    (Romans 1:12)

    d. *"not ashamed of the gospel."* (Romans 1:16)

Explain your choice:

6) From verses five, seventeen, and Habakkuk 2:4, what responsibility is the believer called upon to do?

Read Romans 1:18-32

7) What reason does Paul give that men are certainly Aware of God (vv. 19-20) See also Psalm 19:1-6

8) Why does Paul ferociously condemn certain people? (v. 21)

9) According to verses eighteen through twenty, what most convicts a person?

    a.   Other people do it, so this gives me good reason to do it also.

    b.   God is too far away from everyday life to really matter.

    c.   Hey, if you don't get caught, why not?

    d.   God doesn't exist.

10) Many verses here deal with God's anger, but one verse prompts God to *give them over to judgment*. Select that one. See Exodus 20:4-5, Deuteronomy 4:15-19

    _____ Sinful Acts: _____ Unrighteousness: _____ Idols

11) How many times does *give them over to judgment* appear? _____

Discussion:

"Do not condemn and you will not be condemned." (Luke 6:37) Given the Bible's teachings on judging people, reconcile Paul's critical statements about others.

12) Laws now make same-sex marriage legal. Its proponents cite that Jesus came in love and called upon us to *love one another.* Did Jesus reverse Old Testament Law on the issue of same-sex marriage? (vv. 26-28) See Leviticus 18:22, 20:13, Mark 10:6-8

13) Why might it benefit you and me to understand the depravity of man?

Summary Statement:

Man's need and God's provision! Because of men's depraved nature, self-effort for redemption was futile. Paul immediately teaches that only by full confidence on Divine Provision in the person of Jesus Christ can men live victoriously.

Christianity is not about good conduct! If that were so, then Paul's message of redemption would center on the achievement of human goodness. Let's be clear, Christianity is about Grace! The focus is God's goodness alone! The Apostle is going to talk about Grace and the power of the Cross for the next eight chapters. It is not until Chapter 12 does the Apostle shift to human conduct. And even then, conduct is the result of redemption and not the reverse.

In order to know how precious Grace is, you have to know how bad sin is! And Paul is up to the task. He delivers such a stinging indictment of mankind (vv. 18-32) that he is surely speaking about people of the other political party. To borrow from an illustration of J. Vernon McGee; One bad wintery Sunday morning, a single man is the only person present in church. Still, the preacher delivers his forty minute sermon on the subject of sin. Looking around at all the empty seats, the man asks himself who the preacher might be talking about because he was the only one there!

Paul is not speaking so much about what people do but what the human heart is capable of doing! Consider the resources men spend to deceive and to kill. If Paul were more tender about sin, might not our thinking about our own sins be shallow?

The Good News is; the Gospel has made it possible for God to accept the sinner! That doesn't mean that God's attitude concerning sin has changed. It hasn't. All Judgment will be compared to the Law just as it was in the Old Testament. More Good News, Christ has taken our failings upon Himself. All who accept this pardon are cleared of all wrong doing, past, present and future.

Think about it. The thief on the cross was declared unfit to live in the Roman Empire and so was executed! But Jesus pardoned him, telling him he would make him fit for Heaven. Beloved, that is some pardon! Without Baptism, works, or religious ritual, this thief was saved because he acknowledged Jesus as Lord! (Luke 43:42 NKJV)

Jesus's death was more than about Heaven or hell. His death tore the curtain that once separated all but the Levite Priesthood from God. (Matthew 27:51) No longer was animal sacrifice necessary to approach God. Jesus, the Lamb of God, was the Perfect Sacrifice once and for all. He became our High Priest in the order of Melchizedek. (Hebrews 7:11-17) He is there now, before the Throne of Heaven, interceding for us.

Application

<u>God has a plan for your life, but then, so does the devil</u>. The Revelation of Jesus Christ is a marvelous truth! But is useful only after <u>we receive Him</u>. (Question One)

Perhaps in your study of Romans, Scripture will reveal an area of your life that needs changing, or at least tweaking. Sometimes people choose to ignore sinful ways simply because they have become too comfortable in them. Beloved, if you grieve the Spirit in an area of your life, pray the Lord to reveal it to you and give you the strength to overcome it. Jesus said, *"I have overcome the world."* (John 16:33) Whatever sin you are a slave to, freedom is as close as your knees to the floor.

Notes for Romans 1

Do you sometimes think salvation or maybe some part of it must be earned? If so, either you do not understand Grace or you just can't let go of the idea that we must surely earn something. Grace is confirmed in three word, "It is finished." All you have to do is place your faith in those three words, nothing more.

Romans 2
Walk the Talk

Paul reveals hypocrisy. Chapter 1 began with the righteousness of God and concluded with the unrighteousness of men. This chapter is an indictment of self-righteous Believers. The subject here is not Salvation, but rather, works that confirm Salvation.

Even though Paul is an Apostle to the Gentiles, much of this chapter chastises Jewish Christians who by their very heritage, have a better grasp on matters of conduct. Unfortunately, they see themselves as superior to their Gentile counterparts. As you read this chapter, understand that circumcision is in reference to a Covenant and has nothing to do with supremacy above others. For us today, wedding rings and water baptism both represent vows of devotion and not license to lord one's self over another.

Note: As you read the following verses, circle the word *"you"* and *"yourself."* Above the word Jew, write Christian.

Read Romans 2:1-16

1) In the early Church, why would Jewish converts have a head-start to conduct themselves in a way that could bring discredit upon God and the Christian Faith?

2) In a word, what does Paul reveal in verse one? _____

3) Armed with the knowledge of God's kindness, how might one be led to repentance?

4) We surely realize it is the blood of Jesus that saves. But still, what is the role of good works? (vv. 5-11)

5) What does James 2:26 have to say about works?

Note: To offer a more enlightened answer, take time to read James 2:14-26

6) What does 2 Peter 1:5-10 add to James's oracle about works?

7) What does Paul promise for the self-seeking and those who pay their bills with salacious money? (vv. 8-9)

8) Compare verse twelve with Revelation 20:11-15

Discussion:

"What a man sows, so that shall he reap." (Galatians 6:7-9) *"When you sow, you do not plant the body that will be, but just a seed. <u>God gives it a body he has determined</u>, and to each kind of seed he gives its own body."* (1 Corinthians 15:37-38)

Like believers, unbelievers are given immortal bodies also. Bodies designed to withstand lava fire without ever burning up. They too can never die. (Luke 16:19-31) Do you have a problem with people being thrown into a lake of fire for all Eternity? (Revelation 14:11)

9) Compare verse fifteen with Revelation 17:15-17

Read Romans 2:17-29

10) Is <u>styling</u> representative of <u>engineering</u>? What do you think a question like this means? Think of a movie set in your answer.

11) How many times does the word *Law* appear and why might it be used so much?

12) What do you think it means to hide behind religious ritual? (vv. 25-29)

13) Do you think God will judge self-righteous and religious folks at a higher standard? _____ See Luke 12:48b NKJV

Summary Statement:

Luke 12:48b NKJV confirms, God will judge self-righteous and religious folks on a higher standard. Why? God has given them His Word and His Son! When His people sin, the Spirit is grieved. Worse, the Cross of Christ is disgraced when Christians are observed living outside the framework of Jesus' teachings.

Many profess Christ whose lifestyles, behaviors, even their occupations don't wash. We are not speaking of occasional lapses but lives dedicated to debasing others with malicious rumor, fear, divisiveness and irritating quarrelsomeness. Debasing elected leaders is not the work of the Sprit! Neither is deception, salacious profiteering or self-serving acts. This seems like an endless list but friends, this is the un-regenerated human heart of which the Apostle speaks.

On another front, the Apostle speaks of not using Christianity to lord one's self over others. To the contrary, Christianity is for the purpose of displaying a servant's heart. Being examples of devotion to the One on whom all believers rest their faith. When properly carried out, the fruit of the Spirit is produced; *"love, joy, peace, patience, kindness, goodness, faithfulness, gentleness and self-control."* (Galatians 5:22-23)

Apparently Paul must have had some indication that Jewish converts were lording themselves over their Gentile counterparts. The suggestion that circumcision is at issue confirms this. To put hypocrisy in today's perspective, it would be a Christian who is intolerant of anyone who <u>sins differently than they do</u>. This can easily lead to considering one's self having a superior faith. Not so says Paul. Sin is sin.

Paul also addresses those who think just because they are a good person, they will escape hell! Certainly that would be the case if Salvation were based upon being compared to others. But that method leaves God completely out! These folks falsely believe as Pastor John Hagee puts it; "They think they can make the deal but God says, this is the deal." All men will be compared to Christ who fulfilled the Law.

Who among us can measure up? *"For all have sinned and fall short of the Glory of God."* (Romans 3:23) But in John 3:16, hope has been given whereby men are saved! Jesus fulfilled every aspect of the Law for us. (Matthew 5:17) <u>Man's mistake is in not comprehending the divide between the ungodliness of men and the Holiness of God.</u>

Verse twenty-two maybe slipped by you thinking it doesn't apply today. *You who abhor idols, do you rob temples?* (Romans 2:22) In the Old Testament, Jews engaged in selling gold and silver objects of idol worship among the people which was forbidden. We shouldn't think for one minute this Old Testament practice has nothing to do with today's New Testament world. The parallels are endless.

Christians ought not to be engaged in vending or promoting anything that would be inappropriate to display at the front of your church. In other words, Christians should not be making their living by salacious means. To spell it out, if your daily ventures are laced with sin, the Apostle categorically calls you a hypocrite! Jesus' teachings about hypocrisy is clear enough that all Christians need to endeavor to avoid it.

The Law of Moses had been handed down through generations of Jews. So it would seem their behaviors would exceed Gentile Christians. It seems obvious from Paul's tone, he has information or suspects Jewish Christians are dishonoring the faith more than their Gentile brothers and sisters. Paul even reminds his readers a time is coming when Gentile Christians will be a participant with Christ in matters of Judgment. Even to judging angels. (1 Corinthians 6:2-3) For the Jew, this would not set well.

"A man is not a Christian if he is only one outwardly."
"A man is a Christian if he is one inwardly"
Translated from Romans 2:29

Application

To apply this chapter of Romans to our lives, in truth we must consider our present condition and our path going forward. Anything that doesn't grow withers and dies. Therefore, remain in engaged in the things Christians do. Go to church. Attend a Bible study. The group may not be jaw-dropping perfect but then who among us is? Certainly personal Bible reading is encouraged but remember, the Holy Spirit was given to a Community. God intends for His people to assemble on a regular basis. And finally, does our lifestyle mirror the world or does our walk of faith reflect the teachings of Christ?

Whatever is past is forgiven for the born again Christian! In numerous cases, every person in the early Church had a sordid past. But now they are saved. This is a testimony to the power of the Blood of the Lamb of God. Others may hold grudges against you, but they will not matter at the Day of Judgment. You need not fear man's judgment. *"If God is for us, who can be against us."* (Romans 8:31) Folks with grudges against you will be beset with their own problems fending for themselves.

"You must be born again" (John 3:7)

Romans 3
God's Faithfulness - Man's Excess

Like a seasoned attorney, Paul builds his case that Man's illness is not whopping cough, it is sin! Therefore, the cure for man's illness is not in a prescription bottle, it is in God's Divine plan. Israel's failure in regard to the Law is not representative of God failing. To the contrary, Israel's failure stresses the need for God to do for man what man cannot do for himself.

Read Romans 3:1-8

1) Keying off the word *entrusted* in verse two, write a summary statement which Paul is addressing in the first two verses. Keep in mind, when God spoke to the Hebrew people in the Old Testament, the Church neither existed nor was spoken of.

2) For the Christian today, which of the following truths is the more important?

a. _____ Obedience to the Word b. _____ Abide in the Word c. _____ Study the Word

Explain your choice: See Ezekiel 3:3 and Revelation 10:9-10

3) Is the person who does not believe in Jesus calling God a liar? _____

Discussion:

What do you say to those who only believe Jesus was nothing more than a good teacher and a moral man? Why might God be insulted at such thinking?

4) If God is glorified by His Grace, what is Paul's argument to refute those who say we should sin even more so that God's Glory is more abundant? (vv. 5-8)

5) Why wouldn't more sin advance the glory of God? See Matthew 4:7

Read Romans 3:9-20

Note as you read, Paul's argues that Jewish converts are no better than their Gentile counterparts.

6) Name the six charges Paul brings against Jews and Gentiles alike. (vv. 9-12)

a.

b.

c.

d.

e.

f.

Discussion:

In verses thirteen through eighteen, in what ways do you agree with Paul's indictment of human kind and in what ways do you disagree.

7) If the Law doesn't save, than what is its purpose? (v. 20)

Read Romans 3:21-31

8) What do you notice about the tone of Paul's message in this section compared to the two previous sections?

9) What does Isaiah 7:14, 52:13-53:12 and Micah 5:2 prophecy about?

10) What is this Good News of which the Apostle speaks? (vv. 21-26)

11) Write down and memorize verse twenty-eight.

Discussion:

Think of religious sects who buy into church-designed-schemes (Schemes may seem harsh, but an antiseptic description serves no one) to be reconciled to God. What are some of those schemes? Who is the author of those schemes? _____

Summary Statement:

To borrow a line from J. Vernon McGee; to hold onto the Law is like a man jumping out of an airplane, instead of taking a parachute, he takes a sack of cement with him!"

"No one will be declared righteous in his sight by observing the law." (Romans 3:20)

If we don't already know it, righteousness with God and righteousness in the world are quite different. Righteousness with God is by means of another person. That person is the Son of God. Righteousness with the world rests solely on one's own efforts such as good works and following the laws of government and institutions.

Paul says that righteousness with God is apart from the Law. (Romans 3:21-22) He correctly states that righteousness with God involves one's faith in the worthiness of Christ having fulfilled the Law for them. (Matthew 5:17) What is the purpose of the Law? To identify sin! Paul says there is no such thing as a good person. (Romans 3:9-18) Well try telling that to some! The case unbelievers and the self-righteous conveniently make is to compare one person to another person. In that sense, certainly there are good people. But God compares all men to a standard of perfection. To be blunt, each of us will be compared to Christ Himself! Now how pure do you come across? Paul says that when God looks down our throat, we are all DOA. Penicillin will not cure us. All of us, including truly good people, intellectuals and even religious people, are incapable of comprehending the Holiness of God!

Paul does us a favor by his un-antiseptic approach to explain the human condition. *Their throats are an open grave. Their tongues practice deceit. The poison of vipers is on their lips. "* (Romans 3:13) This is pretty damning! But beloved, that is a description of the best of our species! Now who thinks they or anyone can good their way out of that description?

Now we know how God sees us! Amazingly, He still loves us! He loved us enough to send His only Son as a sacrifice of Himself, even on a tree. Can anyone turn such a gift down? What a foolish thing to do, yet many do. A Baptist preacher in Dallas made this point to his congregation: "There are no unbelievers in hell." They all believe in Jesus!

To get right with another person requires compromise. To get right with God is a take-it or leave-it proposition. God does not force Salvation. We don't have to be saved. We can turn Salvation down. But consider these words. *"The earth is the Lord's, and everything in it, the world and all who live in it." For he founded it."* (Psalm 24:1-2)

"You are living on My Creation, breathing My air and enjoying My sunshine. It is My water that sustains you. Therefore you will live by My Law. If you fail, I will judge you unto eternal death. But because you are My Creation, I love you and have sent My Son to save you from Judgment. No other way will I accept!" (John 3:16)

Application

What contribution can you and I make to heaven? Would we adorn the place by our presence? J. Vernon McGee writes; "I get the impression from some that heaven is going to be a better place when they get there."

Beloved, be aware, this is one of the criticisms that secular humanists have about Christians. They are given to thinking too highly of themselves and forgetting they too were once lost. Christians aren't better, they are just better off. In this, there is a difference. Paul is very aware of pious thinking Pharisees and well he should, he had been one of them! Therefore, he is emphatic on the subject of hypocrisy.

"For it is by grace you have been saved, through faith and this not from yourselves, it is the gift of God...not by works, so that no one can boast." (Ephesians 2:8-9)

Notes for Romans 3

The *institutional church* is intrinsic in Christian society. Its importance cannot be overemphasized yet, because it is administered by fallible human beings, it is not always perfect. Revelation 2 & 3 attests to this fact. List some ways some (not all) churches accommodate the culture.

Romans 4
Abraham Justified by Faith

We have seen that man is a sinner and separated from his Holy Creator. Rather than abandoning man as a hopeless case, God instigates a plan beginning with Abraham. *"Abraham believed the Lord and it was credited to him as righteousness"* (Genesis 15:6)

To solidify this method of reconciliation, David, the revered King by most Jews is used as Paul's example. Though separated by centuries, both Abraham and David are in the same life boat. Paul assures his readers this boat is still afloat and Christ is at the helm. Paul makes it emphatically clear, Jews and Gentiles alike can seek refuge in the same lifeboat of Faith as David and Abraham.

Read Romans 4:1-17

1) Which of the following two statements best represent God's Grace?

   a. Even as we add to our sins, God saves those who love the Lord.

   b. God will save all people whose works deserve the reward of Heaven.

2) How can we tell that Paul is specifically targeting Jewish converts in his opening address of this chapter?

3) How were both Abraham and David reconciled to God? (v. 3) See Psalm 32:5

4) What is Paul's message to the Jews in verse nine and ten?

5) Compare circumcision to present-day water baptism at your church. (vv. 10-11)

6) What is Paul's message to Gentile converts in verse eleven?

7) What relationship links Jewish converts with Gentile converts? (vv. 11-13)

8) What is the principal difference between Faith and the Law? (vv. 14-15)

Discussion:

Using space in your Notes Section of this lesson, list how Faith and Grace are connected? Do not hurry as you <u>share your answer with others</u>. We can learn a great deal from others. It is important everyone fully understands Grace.

Read Romans 4:18-25

9) Compare the quote in verse eighteen with Genesis 1:3, 6, 9, 11, 14, 20, 24.

10) Who is the *"us"* in Genesis 1:26?

11) Compare verse nineteen with Ephesians 2:4-5 and Colossians 2:13?

12) What can you do that Abraham did regarding your own Salvation? (vv. 20-21)

13) Describe the specific power that God used to assure you your Faith is not futile? (vv.24- 25)

Personal Fine-tuning:

God bless you if you believe upon the Lord Jesus. We read in verse twenty that Abraham increased in faith. What things can you do that would give added strength to your faith? (Share with others only if you are comfortable to do so.)

Summary Statement:

Certainly first century Jewish Christians had concern for the Salvation of family members who had passed away before Christ. This chapter puts them to rest that Abraham <u>paid it forward</u> for them, so to speak, until Christ sealed the Covenant.

The Apostle's point in this chapter centers on Faith. A Faith based on God's proven track record regarding Abraham. <u>Israel as a nation would never have come into existence without the power of God</u>. Abraham's and Sarah's bodies were dead to the chance of birthing new life. But by the power of God through Abraham's belief, what was dead brought forth new life. That life was the son of promise, Isaac. <u>Abraham's belief paid it forward</u> for the rest of his people who trusted God until the Resurrection of Christ. This explains why believing Gentiles are called children of Abraham. (Galatians. 3:7, 29)

Does this mean all Jews from the time of Abraham are saved? Absolutely not! *"For not all who are descended from Israel are Israel. Nor because they are his descendants are they all Abraham's children."* (Romans 9:6-7) Paul explores this further in chapters nine, ten and eleven. The Old Testament reveals two kinds of Hebrews, those who looked to God and those who looked to idols and pagan nations.

This is how significant Faith is. <u>Abraham was before the Law</u>. In him the seed of Israel was justified by Faith centuries ahead of the Law given to Moses at Mount Sinai. This is the premise of Paul's case to assure Jews that family members who were deceased before the time of Christ would be saved. In other words, through Christ, God's Grace reaches all the way back to Abraham. In fact, God's Grace was demonstrated in preserving Noah and his family during the flood.

So we ask ourselves this question. How could a Holy and Just God just forget about law-breaking? Is that even lawful? In our system of justice, if our judges did that, society would have serious problems. But <u>God didn't set aside punishment</u>! He simply put it upon Himself for all generations. Isaiah wrote; *"He was pierced for our transgressions."* (Isaiah 53:5) To God be the Glory, Amen

Application

Nothing has changed. The righteousness credited to Abraham resulted in his faith in God's power to birth new life by the birth of his son Isaac. That same power is available to all who have faith in God's plan of Redemption; to birth a born-again child of God.

Notes for Romans 4

Romans 5
The First and Last Adam

<u>This chapter can be complex for the novice Bible student</u>. If this describes you, take a lesson from the account of Philip and the Ethiopian eunuch in the Book of Acts. *"Do you understand what you are reading?" Philip asked. "How can I unless someone explains it to me?"* (Acts 8:30-31)

<u>The Christian life has a dual nature</u>. Find out what it means to be complete, yet still growing; or both bold and humble in coming to God. Understand from God's perspective why one man's sin contaminated humans for all time! Know why we feel the presence of both the Holy Spirit and sin. Or, how can it be Christians are simultaneously heirs and servants? How was Christ both <u>a King</u> and <u>a Servant</u>? If we are not familiar in these complex things, this chapter and others to follow can become <u>just word reading</u>. Meditate on the verses and even ask questions not presented here.

Read Romans 5:1-5

1) What determines if a man or woman is at peace or war with God?

2) What is the message of James 4:4?

3) What does having access to God mean to us that acquits us from Judgment? (v. 2) See John 5:15, Galatians 4:5-7.

Read Romans 5:6-11

4) Write down and memorize verse eight.

5) Select the only thing that justifies a sinner before God.

   a. Excellent church attendance and Bible study

   b. Service to one's church such as preaching, teaching, singing in the choir

   c. Water Baptism

   d. Being a good person and helping those in need

   e. The blood of Jesus, the Lamb of God

6) Explain why the blood of Jesus saves? See Revelation 7:14

7) What is the message of Hebrews 4:14-16?

Read Romans 5:12-21

8) What is God's penalty for sin? (v. 12) See Genesis 2:17, 3:19

9) How did sin and death enter the world and through whom did it enter? See Genesis 2:15-17, 3:6-7, 16-19

10) Using Ephesians 2:3, relate Adam and Eve's actions to what people do today.

11) How does the Apostle Paul contrast Adam and Christ? (vv. 18-19)

Discussion:

Consider verse eighteen where one man brought condemnation to all men. <u>What message would you be sending</u> to your children if, as a parent, you grounded all your children because one child violated his Saturday night curfew? Do you believe this to be a proper way for a parent to teach children that the sin of one affects many?

12) Using a dictionary, define the word *impute* and how it relates to both Adam and Christ.

Summary Statement:

Through the <u>first Adam,</u> sin and death was apportioned to all men. The sin of one man affected all. Through Christ, (the last Adam) sin was pardoned unto eternal life.

Think about it. Sin is never personal, it is shared. In his book, "The Road to Character," author David Brooks centers his hypothesis on two types of Adam. The first Adam type of man is guided by the external. He is a man of works. He aims to get the better of others. Therefore, he is *predisposed to being unprincipled*. The second Adam type is guided by the internal. He seeks *the common good*. Guided by the internal, he is compelled to being principled. Of the two, he is the better servant.

The Apostle Paul writes also of two Adams in his First Epistle to the Corinthians. So the idea of two Adams for this chapter is not too far off the rails. This chapter looks at the last Adam (Christ) and what He brings to the table.

If we read Isaiah 24:5 and Hosea 6:7 we find that a Covenant existed between Adam and God. The Covenant was on the subject of works. God assigned Adam to do and not do certain things. For us today that is the Ten Commandments! But Adam took it upon himself to do his own thing! For that, God was most displeased. Adam's disobedience was the first work of sin. Like all works of sin, many are affected.

Unless you are a most unusual man or woman, you have bent or broken one of God's laws and God has a charge against you. And if God has a charge against you, for certain He is going to find you guilty. So when you stand in Judgment, who will be your advocate, you or Christ? (Revelation 20:11-15) If you know people who don't believe this is going to happen, don't listen to anything they say because they are either ignorant or just plain defiant. Neither of which is a good idea when you are laid out in a box. The real reason for unbelief is they are like the first Adam, they just love having things their way too much to repent of their belief.

Verse twenty emphasizes the growing need for Redemption. As we create potholes in our walk of Faith, the need for repair increases. Paul says Christ is up to the challenge. We may be more technological advanced than the first Adam, but we still have his rebellious nature. We create a lot of potholes! Yes, we have some good works that are godly in every respect. Still, we will be adjudicated to the standard of God's perfect Law fulfilled by just one man. Paul makes it clear, Christ, being that one man, is up to the task that we be pardoned.

To God be the Glory. The measure of His Mercy is endless for those who believe in the One who was sent to save. Amen.

Application

Adam blames God for his own failures. *"The man said, "the woman you put here with me – she gave me some fruit from the tree and I ate it." Then the Lord God said to the woman, "what is this you have done?"* (Genesis 3:12-13)

Think again on this. Sin isn't personal, it is shared! Like Adam, like Jesus, all of us impute something of ourselves onto other people. <u>Adam imputed sin onto us all</u>. Therefore, without Christ, a man stands condemned!

Our Sanctification commands us to not impute sinful works as did Adam. To do so affects everyone around us and sometimes beyond the present. Sanctification is much like a plant or tree, fruit is delivered. As plants and trees require occasional nourishment, so too the Christian life requires nourishment. In addition to solitary study of God's Word, it is essential for believers to never cease gathering. Gathering with God's people gives us an <u>abiding Spirit</u>. *"He who abides in me, and I in him, bears much fruit."* (John 15:5 NKJV)

Notes for Romans 5

Romans 6
Understanding the Holiness of God

Since the fall of man, all humans come into the world in a state of unrighteousness. (Psalm 51:5) Still it remains, until we come to terms with seeing sin for what it is, understanding it <u>from God's perspective</u> is impossible.

In this chapter, Paul says that at birth, every inch of the human body from the head to the feet are up for grabs. To rephrase this, <u>every part of our body is going to respond to what it loves most</u>. Therefore Paul tells us, all people are slaves to something or to someone. In short, we each are either controlled by righteousness or unrighteousness. Graciously, God makes what is unrighteous righteous by means of a simple act of belief. In an instant, what was once dead becomes alive.

Read Romans 6:1-14

1) If sin can no longer send the believer to hell, why not just continue in sin? (v. 2)

2) Paul states that the believer is dead to sin. But still, all believers frequently sin. Select the word that best describes what Paul is talking about.

Circle one: Lifestyle   Baptism   Authority   Repentance

3) If we are united with Christ in death, we are also united with Him in His resurrection. What badge do we wear indicating both death and Resurrection?

Circle one: Tithing   Baptism   Lord's Supper   Church attendance

4) Paul has a real concern some people may view Grace as a license to sin. What dangers are there for individuals with such a mindset? See 2 Timothy 3:5

5) What offering are believers to give to God? (v. 13) See also Micah 6:6-8.

Read Romans 6:15-23

6) What is a slave?

7) In the context Paul is speaking, believers and unbelievers alike are all slaves; serving something or someone.

a. Whom do unbelievers serve? _____

b. Whom do believers serve? _____

8) When you observe a believer engaged in selfish living, what comes to mind? See Revelation 2:4 and Luke 11:33

9) Would you say this to be true? All are slaves to what they love most? _____

10) Combine the messages of Matthew 6:24 and 1 Timothy 6:10.

11) Would you agree with the message of the following Scriptures? Yes or No:

Matthew 6:1-9   Photo Opt Christianity _____

2 Corinthians 6:14-17   Plant, Grow, Bear Fruit _____

Ephesians 4:25-28   Do not give the devil a beachhead in your life _____

Ephesians 4:29-32   Do not grieve the Spirit _____

Hebrews 4:14   We should approach God with trembling _____

Discussion:

The magnitude of God's Grace: In this chapter, we have noted that we are speaking of adult accountability. The question often comes up, what about infants, the newborn or the unborn. <u>They have not reached the age of accountability</u>. Does God send them to hell? 2 Samuel 12:18-23 and Matthew 18:10 may shed some light on this question.

Summary Statement:

"Surely I was sinful at birth, sinful from the time my mother conceived me."
Psalm 51:5

"Even from birth the wicked go astray;
from the womb they are wayward and speak lies."
Psalm 58:3

This verse isn't just about pedophiles, serial rapists and killers. It is speaking of *all* who deny Christ. To deny Jesus is a lie! Shifting guilt is a lie. (Genesis 3:12) In God's eyes, <u>any form of separation from His *Authority* is unrighteousness</u>. (Question two)

Sadly, the expression unrighteousness doesn't really ring so badly to us. That is because of our casual concept of the word. Sin is pretty much an unacceptable word in modern culture. People simply don't want to hear of it or about it!

From Chapter 5, we have said understanding Scripture can be complex. Even our good works are sin! How you ask? – When a nonbeliever does a good work, he, not God is praised! Jesus affirms this; *"apart from me you can do nothing."* (John 15:5) God is jealous when something or someone other than Himself is glorified apart from Him. (1 Corinthians 6:20) <u>Glorifying of self is tantamount to admiration of an idol</u>. Many people are just simply stuck on themselves. They are the arrogant and the proud. Beloved, passages warning against both are endless!

Adam's work signaled we are a rebellious species. This is the perspective of a Holy God. *"<u>All of us</u> have become like one who is unclean, and all our righteous acts are like filthy rags"* (Isaiah 64:6) Granted, the context of this passage refers to pre-Babylonian Israel. But even this Prophet of God Isaiah, is inclusive of himself and from this <u>we must conclude</u>, the whole of mankind is tainted and estranged from God! John 3:16 confirms this truth that <u>the whole world is culpable in depravity</u>. The doctrine of total depravity is also taught elsewhere in Scripture. (Ephesians 2:1-5)

Isaiah used the Hebrew word *"iddah"* in his description of *filthy rags*. We call this today a discarded feminine product. We can't make it any clearer our need for Christ. Standing naked and alone on our works is not a good plan. (Genesis 3:7-11, Revelation 3:17)

So why do good works? Apart from Christ, the world identifies with you and rewards you. Being justified in the Son, we now become identified with the Father who rewards us. (Matthew 13:44-45) Which is better? By the one act, (The Cross) works become a matter of our Sanctification. There is a <u>new Authority</u> in our life! <small>(Again, question two)</small> Having died to self, God is glorified by one's good deeds.

Keep in mind, Justification was a single act. <u>Sanctification is an endeavor of continuing work</u>, free of work-stoppages. Justification takes place in the instant we take Christ into our life as Lord and Savior. It is at this point all guilt is removed and we can *boldly approach* our heavenly Father in all areas of righteousness.

Application

Citing 1 John 4:8, the Universalists contend God is too loving to send anyone to hell. They conveniently omit verses nine and ten following verse eight. Such thinking dismisses the Holiness and Justice of God. In fact, it dismisses the entire Book of Revelation, the Parables of Jesus and His Olivet Discourse.

Constructively, you don't have to murder your neighbor to go to hell. Neither do we have to be so extreme as to deny the existence of God. There are more conventional ways to end up in hell. To continue in sin is the path of most according to Paul. Paul reasons that <u>to continue in sin is to be a slave to it</u>! Paul makes his case that in Christ, the old has died and the new is born. It is at this point, the believer becomes a slave for righteousness.

It is to this end we come to recognize that our <u>righteous acts</u> come as a result of God within us. In this way, God receives the glory and not ourselves. God can say to the devil, "See this good thing my child does."

Notes for Romans 6

Romans 7
New Life – Master – Love, Old Struggles

Two perspectives accompany this chapter. First, the passing of the bonds of Law to a bond of love and second, an illustration of good intentions and hopeless frustration. What the Apostle Paul says of himself might just lead a believer to simply throw up their hands in defeat and anticipate living a sloppy and frustrating life. But Paul outlines how assigning one's self to Christ gives way to the joy of knowing we live under His authority and not the authority of the Law. It is at this point we need not be frustrated, because our failures become fewer. Further, the failures that do occur, Christ has us covered. It doesn't get any better than that!

Read Romans 7:1-12

1) What leads us to understand this Apostle is dead serious that it is imperative that all who read his writings reach correct conclusions about the Faith? (v. 1)

2) How might one's mind, even whole personality change knowing that we have replaced serving a set of rules with serving a loving person?

3) How is it that the Christian can die to the Law? (v. 4)

4) With use of a dictionary, define authority.

5) Explain the difference between being under the authority of the Law and under the authority of Christ.

6) Write down and memorize the fruit of God? See Galatians 5:22-23

7) If a man has many things of God but has not love, how is he described? (1 Corinthians 13:1)

8) Do you think the Church is right to sweep wrongdoing under the carpet so as not to damage the image of the Faith? _____ See Ephesians 5:10-11

Discussion:

What might be some pros and cons of publicly exposing serious wrongdoing in the Church?

9) How do we identify what sin is? (v. 7)

10) If the Law cannot save a sinner, is it no longer Holy? _____ (v. 12)

Read Romans 7:13-25
11) What is Paul's point in verse fifteen?

Discussion:
Do you agree with those who say, if you are in Christ, it is impossible to commit a sin?
What do you say to a person with such thinking?

12) According to Psalm 51:1-2, list words that describe the nature of God and the hope
of a repentant person.

a. _____ d. _____

b. _____ e. _____

c. _____

13) On your notes page, to the best of your ability, paraphrase Paul's words about
himself in verses twenty-one through twenty-five.

14) How does Paul's description of his personal struggle affect your walk of faith?

Discussion:
God gave Paul what is described as a thorn in his flesh. (2 Corinthians 12:7) From your
reading of 2 Corinthians 12:7-10, what do you conclude this thorn to be? (See Overview)

Summary Statement:
The Law may not save us, but still, it is extremely useful in that, it reveals how we have
a need. Because, in spite of our best intentions, there is a power in each of us working
to take us down. See 1 Peter 5:8

This is one of those good news bad news chapters. Fortunately, the good news dominates. It is clear, good intentions never did anything good as long as the individual leads a divided life. Paul's experience alone tells us even with the new nature, the old nature sabotages good intentions. And it is because of this, Paul reiterates not to place our trust in ourselves to be a model Law-keeper. Because the Law cannot save even the best of law-keepers! Judging from Paul's concerns, it is apparent the concept of being a good Law-keeper was at work in the Church at Rome. This congregation displayed good intentions by gathering together in the name of Christ, but they weren't really quite ready just yet to let go of the Law.

This problem was not unique to the early Church. Many today have good intentions to serve Christ and to love Him and so they feel warm singing *"I Surrender All."* But two problems exists. They either don't have the power to let go of legalism or, they have things they just simply love too much to let them go. (See Luke 18:22-28)

Paul uses marriage as a tool to teach that a love bonded relationship is superior to a Law binding contract. Whereas the Law condemns us for default and therefore death, Christ absolves our default and frees us from default's condemnation! The bond of love appeals to the heart whereas the bond of Law appeals to our head. It is better to give one's heart to the Lord than our head to a set of regulations. And when motives change, our view of the world changes. The world says live for self. But God says to live for the glory of the Lord. He didn't create us for us, He created us for His glory.

The subject often comes up about Paul's thorn and what it was. Here it is in this chapter. It was his sin nature! *"My grace is sufficient for you."* (2 Corinthians 12:9) Any suggestion of Paul's thorn being a speech impediment, a club foot or anything physical is just silly and wrong! Who would need Grace for a physical defect? Paul needed mercy for the same reason you and I need mercy, our sin nature. The full story of Paul's thorn is revealed in 2 Corinthians 12:7-10.

Relating to one question, it is hypocritical to sweep wrongdoing under the rug so as to pretend wrongdoing is not in the Church. The Church is after all, full of sinners and wrongdoers. To pretend the Church is perfect is to not understand righteousness. Righteousness is in the work of Jesus and not the work of men!

People expect, and therefore respect, institutions who initiate cleaning their own house. <u>It should not be up to the unchurched to clean the Church</u>! At the preparation of this lesson, a prominent Denominational Institution of higher learning, after some years of delay, cleaned its own house regarding athletes sexually assaulting women. Those who chose to look the other way were dismissed by a responsible Board of Regents. The integrity of the school's Regents upheld the Faith! Because of that, a deeper respect for the Faith resulted. Of course we in the Church are not perfect! <u>We shouldn't pretend we are</u>.

For some reason, Christian institutions seem to want to appear perfect. Image motivates sweeping wrong-doing under the rug. To do so is hypocritical. It is far nobler for the Church to clean its own house than ultimately be exposed as hypocrites by secular media. Making amends is the convicting work of the Holy Spirit.

Application

Beware of two traps! Good intentions and comparative goodness. <u>Good intentions are simply placebos</u>, the devil's deception if you will! Good intentions give-off warm feelings of goodness but the reality is, nothing is ever delivered; meaning to say, <u>delivered unto Jesus</u>. Think of it this way, Christ wants you to deliver yourself to Him, both in body and in Spirit! (See Luke 18:22-28)

Second, <u>comparative goodness</u>. This is the devil <u>scratching your ego</u>. Never get caught-up in comparing one's own goodness to others. Beloved, Christians aren't better, they are just better-off!

Notes for Romans 7

Romans 8
Victorious Living

<u>The first verse of this chapter is the embodiment of Christianity.</u> Christianity 101 if you will. Christ is summed up. Sanctification is clear and future glory is announced! The liberation of God's children from the decay of the present earth for which the Creation groans, has taken place. All the result of one single event. If one only had time to read one chapter of Romans, this one stands out.

There is a treasure-trove of memory verses for every Christian to grasp in this chapter.

Read Romans 8:1-17

1) Write down and memorize verse one.

2) What has Christ Jesus done for those who believe upon Him? (v. 2)

3) Why is the Law powerless to save you? (v. 3)

4) What did God do regarding the Law's requirement of a sin offering? (vv. 3-4)

5) Explain the different mindset of believers and nonbelievers. (v. 5)

6) What is the destiny of those who do not please God? (vv. 6-8)

7) Explain the differing conditions of the body with the Spirit and the body without the Spirit. Having once received the Spirit, what responsibility follows? (vv. 9-12)

8) To what can the person who lives by the Spirit lay claim? (vv. 13-17)

Read Romans 8:18-27

9) What can we anticipate one day happening? (vv. 19-21) See also Revelation 21:1

10) If we follow up on verse twenty-two, we understand in simple terms how the Creation will come to groaning. How for example, will cattle experience groanings? See Joel 1:18 and Revelation 8:7

11) If you feel a call to pray but are not sure how to direct your prayer, should you skip the prayer all together or take another course? (vv. 26-27)

Read Romans 8:28-39

12) Write down and memorize verse twenty-eight.

13) What was God's plan from the beginning? (vv. 29-30)

14) What is the Good News of verses thirty-one through thirty-three?

15) Compare verse thirty-four with Hebrews 7:24-28.

16) Write down and memorize verses thirty eight and thirty nine.

Summary Statement:

"There is now no condemnation for those who are in Christ Jesus." (v. 1)

If a person was only going to read one chapter of Romans, it should be this chapter.

After carefully reading the chapter, all we can do is simply stand as Moses did at the burning bush and just <u>marvel at the glory and wonder of Salvation</u>.

This chapter is the summation of the first seven. Think about it. Since Adam, the destiny of every newborn is condemnation unto death. *"For dust you are and to dust you will return."* (Genesis 3:19) Simply left to ourselves with this verse, we would be without hope. In that declaration, the Creator put all mankind on a death watch.

In Chapter 7, Paul raises a question that all of us should ask. *"Who will rescue me from this body of death?"* (Romans 7:24) The answer is in this chapter. Paul begins the chapter with one of the most glorious verses in all the Bible. *"There is now no condemnation for those who are in Christ Jesus."* (Romans 8:1) He builds upon this pronouncement with the promise of future glory and complete victory. Maranatha!

In mercy, the Creator has taken pity on us and provided a way to escape the Perdition watch-list. In one single act of Grace, God sacrificed His Son on a tree as ransom for sin for all who receive Him. *"And by Him we cry "Abba" Father."* (Romans 8:15)

It isn't just people going to be redeemed, <u>the whole of Creation is going to be redeemed from decay</u>. The Creation groans as in childbirth. (Romans 8:22) Living in a world of hate, violence and bigotry, believers also groan as they await the Lord's return. At this lesson's preparation, there is news of twenty-two bomb threats in thirteen states against Jewish institutions. This follows upon the heels of significant vandalism at Jewish burial sites in two states. And America is a champion of Israel!

Though it goes unnoticed, there are decaying stars and planets dying daily along with one-hundred fifty-thousand plus people on earth. A day is coming when all decay and dying will cease and *all* things will be redeemed, that is, replaced with a new and never decaying Creation. Imagine this if you will. *"I saw a new heaven and a new earth." "He will wipe away every tear from their eyes. There will be no more death or mourning or crying or pain."* (Revelation 21:1, 4)

This chapter closes with two of the most assuring verses in all the New Testament. If these two verses are planted in our mind and our heart, whatever <u>weakness we display</u>, whatever the news brings, whatever our family or our doctor conveys, we can rest with confidence. <u>God's love for us is unfailing</u>.

Application

<u>Only a life lived in the Spirit is pleasing to God</u>. It is not until the Spirit awakens us, do we tune into God's will. Decisions made without regard to His will is like an aircraft with neither compass nor altimeter. It ultimately crashes and burns.

Therefore, as a Christian, let us not be guided by the will of what the flesh desires. Instead, be guided by the Spirit, going about doing the right things to His Glory.

"Let your light shine before men,
that they may see your good deeds
and praise your Father in heaven."
Matthew 5:16

"Do nothing out of selfish ambition or vain conceit, but in humility
consider others better than yourselves.
Each of you should look not only to your own interests,
but also to the interest of others.
Your attitude should be the same as that of Christ Jesus."
Philippians 2:3-5

Notes for Romans 8

Chapter 12 follows Chapter 8 quite nicely. That is how this study is presented. If you prefer, you may follow the order of your Bible and go now to Chapter 9.

Romans 12
Supernatural Living

We switch now from the inner *being* to the outer *being*. Christian Doctrine for the first eight chapters gives way to Christian living. Boots on the ground if you will. God has good, pleasing and perfect plans for those who enlist into his service. The mission; <u>being visible for His Glory</u>.

Beginning with Paul's Doxology of praise for God's plan of Salvation for both Jew and Gentile, (Romans 11:33-36) we come to understand what it is to become a living sacrifice.

Read Romans 11:33-36

1) Do you think God owes you anything and if so, why?

2) Do you think it appropriate to give God advice?

3) Have you ever given anything to God that maybe put Him in the awkward position of owing you something in return?

4) What do you have that God has not given you?

Read Romans 12:1-8

5) What do you think are the greatest obstacles to living a life pleasing to the Lord?

6) Compare verse one with Leviticus 16:11-16

7) Is a renewed mind necessary to desire to do God's will? See 1 Corinthians 2:14

8) What is Paul's suggestion for the person high on their own religious self? (v. 3)

9) Do you believe Christians to be better people than non-Christians?

Note: See the Application, paragraph two, of the lesson on Romans Chapter Seven.

Discussion:

Dangerously, there exist in the world today, fanatic religions who believe anyone outside their religion are unworthy of God. Sadly, some sects of Christianity have the same view minus the violence. Do you think these sects assume a superiority?

10) What is the message of verse five?

Discussion:
Describe the changes in yourself from the time before you were saved to the time following receiving Christ into your life. What do you say to the person who says nothing changed and how do you say it?

Read Romans 12:9-21
11) In your own words, how would you describe supernatural living?

12) Does *love* suggest emotional feelings or hands-on action? See 1 John 3:16-18

13) Why is it important to persevere in difficult times? See James 1:2-4

14) It is difficult to evaluate others because unlike God, we do not see the heart. Yet, there are times we must. What tools does God give us to access trustworthiness? See Amos 7:7-8 and Matthew 7:16

15) How are verses seventeen and nineteen contrary to the worldview?

Discussion:
Why is revenge attractive? Understanding that Scripture condemns revenge, how might we find satisfaction in refraining from getting revenge?

16) What two tools does God make available for supernatural living? See Psalm 119:105 and John 14:26

Summary Statement:
"Do not conform any longer to the pattern of this world, but be transformed by the renewing of your mind." (Romans 12:2)

"Yet it was the Lord's will to crush him and cause him to suffer.
After the suffering of his soul, he will see the light of life and be satisfied.
By his knowledge my righteous servant will justify many."
(Isaiah 53:10-11 pp)

God was pleased when Jesus shed His blood at the cross. He saw sin take its last breath. Christ didn't die expecting us to do something He hadn't done. He died for us to be something. And that something is a life lived in stark contrast to the world in which we live. That is what this and the following chapters are about.

As a pianist practices daily preparing music for a future performance, so also God wants His people to practice daily in preparation for Kingdom living. To that end, Paul addresses a person's relationship both within and outside the Body of Christ.

If the question were asked; what is the number one reason to read the Bible? Some might answer; to learn about God or for moral guidance. Both sound like seemingly good answers but both would be wrong answers. Beloved, God wants us to *be transformed* into the likeness of His Son! All the facts we can cram into our head and all the good deeds we can rack up are of no use until we are transformed!

There are many who possess biblical knowledge, can quickly recite verse after verse, but whose fruit demonstrate they are not transformed. Paul himself identifies them in his second letter to Timothy. *"People who are lovers of themselves, lovers of money, boastful, proud, abusive, abandon parents, unholy, without love, unforgiving, slanderous, without self-control, brutal, not lovers of good, treacherous, conceited, lovers of pleasure rather than lovers of God – having a form of godliness but denying its power."* (2 Timothy 3:2-5 paraphrased)

Such an example was exhibited by a church attending elderly gentlemen living near an HOA community. Because he displayed a great deal of biblical knowledge, he was invited to join the HOA neighborhood Bible study group as a guest. Whereupon, he targets an elderly female member with inappropriate emails, and harassing phone calls. This is what Paul is addressing. Biblical knowledge is useless without transformation. This individual simply was not transformed. It is what we are, not what Bible verses we can recite! *"You will know them by their fruit."* (Matthew 7:16)

This chapter is inclusive of what Christians refer to as Spiritual gifts. God doesn't want His children to mothball their special abilities, but share their abilities with all.

One of the more difficult things God asks of His children is to be joyful in times of trials. This is because <u>He doesn't want us to be lazy in our Faith.</u> Imagine if you will, a parent who never ask a son to mow the yard or a daughter to wash the dishes. Faith, like any muscle, needs exercise! <u>Trials are God's barbells to strengthen our Faith</u>. The heart as a spiritual muscle in addition to being a physical muscle. Tragedies happen so that as we see them, especially feel them, we develop a strong sense of empathy for others. God saw our needs and sent His Son. In like manner we too, as we see the needs of others, send ourselves.

Application

The summary statement was drawn from the text itself. It is accompanied with Paul meticulously contrasting worldly living with Kingdom living. To apply Kingdom living and therefore <u>supernatural living</u>, it is necessary to identify both useful and useless traits in the service of the Faith.

He contrasts being humble as opposed to prideful, generous rather than stingy, loving replacing hatefulness, other-centered superseding me-centeredness, enthusiasm supplanting indifference, bridge-building replacing bridge-burning and forgiveness replacing vengefulness. What of these might you relate to?

Notes for Romans 12

Romans 13
Defiance of Authority is Rebellion against God

This may be difficult, but <u>government need not recognize God to be valid</u>! Indeed, in Paul's time, the worst of the worst governed in Rome and in Israel. Scripture is clear, contempt for government is contempt for the Lord. It is a known fact, even in a pagan culture, the Gospel can take root where civil order is kept.

<u>Love and the golden rule</u>: Certainly our actions speak of love for those close to us. But what about those we may never even meet? Do our dogs continually annoy neighbors or endanger their children? Are your guns secured? We think we understand love but truly, love paints with a broad brush.

"Let no debt remain outstanding." Paul is not talking about credit card debt or bank loans. Neither is he saying don't use credit cards. <u>He is saying</u> to love your neighbor enough to secure dogs and guns. <u>He is saying</u> don't smother children from experiencing some of life's failures. Neither is permissiveness of a child's wrong-doing an act of love.

Read Romans 13:1-7

1) Compare verses one through seven with 1 Timothy 2:1-4.

2) Identify the biblical accounts of the end results of individuals and groups who rebelled against their ruling authority? See Numbers 16:30-33 and 2 Samuel 18:9, 14

3) Under what circumstance would a Christian disobey civil law? See Daniel 6:5-10 and Acts 5:27-32

4) What does Scripture command of ruling authorities?

   a. Proverbs 2:3

   b. Proverbs 29:4

   c. Matthew 20:25a

Discussion:

When the King's law obstructed Daniel's relationship with God, Daniel simply did not obey them. Neither did he take to the streets or organize an armed standoff. What is appropriate Christian response to government laws contrary to God's laws?

Read Romans 13:8-14

5) What debt does the Apostle tell us to never pay off? (v. 8)

6) Compare verse eleven with the Parable of the Ten Virgins? See Matthew 25:1-13

7) The world loves the night life, but what kind of day-life are Christians called upon to engage? (vv. 12-13)

8) What is essential to clothe one's self with Christ? (v. 14)

9) Do you think there is such a thing as overprotective love? Explain?

10) Do you think the <u>ever-present</u> <u>parent</u> is a perversion of love? _____

11) Do you think being permissive is love? _____ Why?

12) Is any and all manner of love always biblical? Explain

13) Is giving of yourself love? Why? (See Application)

14) What is the message of 1 Corinthians 13:1?

Summary Statement:

<u>Citizens of Heaven</u> must honor the authority of the earthly nation they are a sojourner in. During this temporal time, they are to properly love their own and be respecting of others. Love is displayed by doing rather than being limited to emotional feelings.

<u>Civil disorder is the devil's work</u> to disrupt spreading the Gospel – A Federal Building in a large city is bombed; Anti-government extremists refuse to pay taxes because they refuse to accept the federal government; Anti-government extremists threaten federal agents with being shot; The President is an alien is posted on the internet; Pastors pray for the death of the President; Congregations pray for the death of Supreme Court Justices; A Congregation rejoices at the death of an Aids victim; The death of a Gay soldier is cheered; Local sheriffs refuse to enforce gun laws they don't agree with; high state official suggests secession from the Union.

Many perpetrators of civil unrest are Christians who <u>place sedition ahead of the Great Commission</u>. Unwittingly, they become pawns of the devil. The devil knows civil unrest deters advancing the Gospel of Jesus Christ. Seditious acts often follow losing an election. Where is the gratefulness to God to have been born into a country that allows people to vote? Sanctification is the first casualty of civil rebellion.

The human species has to be controlled because all humans are sinners, ungrateful and rebellious lawbreakers! Without civil authorities, <u>even ungodly ones</u>, chaos and anarchy would exist. The Book of Judges testifies to this truth! *"In those days, Israel had no king, everyone did as he saw fit."* (Judges 21:25) Paul says Christian behavior isn't to be checked at the door upon entering city hall.

Think about it. Because <u>Jesus didn't provoke the Jews</u> to attack Roman authority, the Church was born and you and I came to Salvation! To cite one recent example: Iraq was stable under its authoritarian Ruler and the Gospel was alive and well. Then an invasion overthrew its government. The overthrow cost the lives of thousands of Christians living there. <u>It cost the future Salvation of thousands more</u> who would have come to Christ! It set a part of the world ablaze from which the Gospel may never recover. If ever there was a work of the devil, this was it! "The people will view us as liberators" spoke one high official. Rest assured, God didn't agree! These perpetrators of deceit stole Salvation away from thousands. People who are responsible for the deaths of thousands will *surely* reap the whirlwind! (Hosea 8:7)

Those disrespectful of leaders have the <u>Judas syndrome</u> though few would admit it. They existed in Moses' time in the person of Korah and the time of King David by his son Absalom. (Numbers 16, 2 Samuel 15) Their goal was rebellion against authority.

Lawmakers themselves unwittingly rebel against its own-self when controlling members undermine the very constitution they claim to uphold by disallowing voting on issues its majority members oppose.

"A scoundrel and villain, who goes about with a corrupt mouth, who winks with his eye, signals with his feet and motions with his fingers, who plots evil with deceit in his heart – he always stirs up dissension. Therefore disaster will overtake him in an instant; he will suddenly be destroyed without remedy." **(Proverbs 6:12-15)**

<u>Love is not just a matter of emotions or circumstances, but of the *will*.</u> Love of family and friends are emotions. Loving one for a favor or gift is a circumstance. The will to be caring for nameless people is Paul's point. <u>Love will cost you something</u>; be it time or money, something is surrendered. – Clean-up before leaving a picnic area; caring for rental property; controlling pets; securing guns.

An oxymoron for a Christian is loving God and ignoring a parent. Love is a phone call, a card, <u>a time surrendered from self</u>. Indifference to a parent violates one of the staples of the Ten Commandments. It is worse than an unbelief. (1 Timothy 5:8)

Many of the aforementioned are nothing short of bullies. Bullies are pervasive in society. They don't see their victims as precious souls made in God's image. Some live on second floor apartments, drive our streets and serve in leadership positions. They bully because they can! Like their adolescent counterparts, they possess some advantage in wealth, firepower or horsepower. They are often violent road-rage types, aggressive, me-centered and highly entitled. Amazingly, when exposed, they see themselves as the victim. Of such the Scriptures say. *"The ruthless will vanish, the mockers will disappear, and all who have an eye for evil will be cut down."* **(Isaiah 29:20)** Bullies can be Christians. Ourselves if we are not alert. Lording one's self over other believers is certainly a form of bullying. Read Galatians 13:4-7

Love for others *is* the highest motive. <u>Love seeks the best for others</u>. There exists perversions of love such as possessiveness, permissiveness, overprotectiveness or same-sex marriage. Space is limited, but you can identify other perversions of love.

Application

Daniel Webster wrote, "Whatever makes men good Christians makes them good citizens." Prayerfully ask the Spirit to search your heart and reveal attitudes that dishonor the Faith. And remember, <u>love will always cost you something</u>. For Jesus, it was being nailed to a tree. Love is the embodiment of the Ten Commandments.

Romans 14
Those Questionable Grey Areas

Accepting one another is easy as long as the subject is meat and vegetables! – The new pastor is dressed in jeans. Guitars and drums replaced hymnals and robed choir. The musicians smoke in the courtyard between services. The younger set sits to the front while the older folks take the rear pews. The gyrations in the front annoy the older set in the back distracting their focus and purpose for even attending. The younger set is convinced it is the Spirit that moves them. The older set suggests it is the euphoria of the drum beat, the flesh if you will, that moves them. Should the Church prepare to mix the *lawfully wedded* generation with the *live together* generation?

Paul opens a can of worms for us in this chapter by <u>contrasting how people give glory to God</u>. In the scene above, one group feels shackled by traditions resembling legalism while the older group feels threatened by an overreach of *freedom in Christ*. Meat and vegetables in Paul's day; tobacco, rock music, birth control, shorts and sandals today. Some may find comfort in this quote: "It is right for the church to be in the world. It is wrong for the world to be in the church." Harold Lindsell

Read Romans 14:1-11

1) What principles must a church congregation incorporate to stay unified when it comes to accepting their undeniable age differences? See John 13:34 and John 15:12

2) In light of John 19:30, what are the dangers of legalism?

3) In light of James 4:4, what are the dangers of liberalism?

Discussion:

Open a class dialogue that considers *weak* and *strong* faith with *freedom* in Christ on the following subjects.

a. Facial make-up
b. Tattoos
c. Casual dress of men as opposed to coat and tie in church
d. Eating and drinking during a church worship service
e. Those who participate in congregational singing and those who don't
f. Those who prefer electric guitars and drums; those who prefer hymns

g. Those who only go to church on Christmas and Easter

h. The 80/20 rule – 20% contribute 80% of the funds necessary to support Church and missions

4) From 1 Corinthians 15:2-4, what are the non-disputable, essential elements of faith?

5) What is Paul's concern in verse ten?

Read Romans 14:12-23

6) Using something other than the food we eat, what would be a real-world stumbling block? (v. 14-15)

7) Who do you think is the more obligated when weak and strong come together? Explain:

8) Someone somewhere is bound to be offended by almost anything others do. What can we do to apply the principles Paul sets forth in a difficult situation? (vv. 19-22)

9) Do you ever see a time when you would do something you feel is unworthy of a Christian? So for the sake of a relationship you would participate? Consider R rated movies, topless bars, gossip, employing scantily dressed waitresses, doing drugs.

10) Would you be a participant in internet pornographic activity with a friend?

11) Based on 1 Corinthians 10:23-33, what does it mean to glorify God in our works?

Summary Statement:

Differences do not endanger Salvation! *"Blessed is the man who does not condemn himself by what he approves."* (Romans 14:22)

Freedom in Christ has to do with not being under <u>authority of the Law</u>. But it is not a license to sin! *"Do not be deceived; God cannot be mocked. A man reaps what he sows. The one who sows to please his sinful nature, from that nature will reap destruction."* (Galatians 6:7-8)

Paul begins the chapter warning us <u>not to construct our own list of taboos, dos and don'ts if you will, on which we judge others</u>. Certainly Scripture condemns adultery, murder and the like. And we are to judge these things accordingly! But the things in the grey areas such as card playing, tobacco, dancing, tattoos and alcohol that are not specifically addressed in Scripture <u>are a matter of conscience, not Law</u>!

There are some of the Faith that not only embrace the Ten Commandments, they have added ten more! The result is others are judged based on <u>made-up criteria</u>. Most of the new ones are all don'ts. Don't dance, play cards, watch TV, swim in mixed gender settings, use tobacco, drink coffee nor alcohol, cut your hair, wear pants and don't play the saxophone! All of these play into practices of various religious sects and are taken seriously by their followers.

The Apostle says these things are <u>a matter of conscience and have nothing to do with Salvation</u>. As the hymn articulates, Salvation is in Christ Alone. Paul is clear, folks who have not come to full maturity often cling to manmade taboos. The mature believer lives by the Word of God, not taboos. Nevertheless, he is <u>not to condemn the immature believer that is still learning to understand Grace</u>. Both mature and immature share this in common, both make lifestyle choices for the glory of God. And this is to be respected.

Note: Please, let us not make a case for alcohol being a sin based on Scripture. *"Go, eat your food with gladness, and drink your wine with a joyful heart."* (Ecclesiastes 9:7) See also Amos 9:14. No doubt, Scripture is adamant that drunkenness is a sin.

There is a line that separates lifestyle and legalism and <u>it is important to know the difference</u>. If we abstain from alcohol or tobacco as a necessary part for Salvation, that is legalism and just plain heresy. It is a form of Old Testament Judaism if you will, and demonstrates the person is clueless about Salvation and are not yet saved!

For it is by Grace alone one is saved and has nothing to do with rule keeping. Rule keeping is the result of Salvation and not the reverse!

The righteousness that saves comes from above. If our abstentions are a way to honor God, then wonderful! The grey areas of the Bible are not going to send anybody to hell. If that were so, Scripture would warn us. It is heresy and unbelief that people send themselves to hell and on that, the Bible is clear.

Perhaps the anti-alcohol tobacco folks be reminded of a man who spoke often of God without hesitation. Winston Churchill held a cigar in one hand and a brandy in the other when sitting in the dentist's chair. Surely Churchill did not forfeit his soul?

J. Vernon McGee relates of a woman who, after nearly four years in the mission field, returned home a spiritual wreck. She had all the virtues of a Christian. She didn't smoke, drink, play cards, attend movies, dance, use an electric keyboard in worship and she no longer used makeup. What a way to live! Did Jesus come down to earth to have us live like that only to have the Church come along and place such restrictions on us? She seemed to think so. If Christ reigns in our heart, our conduct is going to be fine. Because we are going to practice the law of love. If you are wearing a religious straight jacket demanded by the edicts of some church, take it off because it won't save you. Grace has already saved you! Denominations that tell visiting Christians they can't share Communion because they are not members of their Sect need a heart check and less starch in their self-righteous shirts.

Application

This and the previous chapter are truly connected at the hip. The previous chapter depicts a *left footprint* in the world. This chapter depicts a *right footprint* in the Body of Christ. With hate, violence and bigotry at an all-time high resulting in people judging everyone not agreeing with them, a bath is needed. Perhaps we all need a bath! Not of soap and water but a bath in the Spirit of love.

When God formed me in my mother's womb I was given a birth mark and that is sufficient for me. My body is a temple and my conscience leads me to not desecrate it. Neither do I desire to draw attention to myself or display a graven image that suggests a love for it. But I am not going to pass judgment on tattoos. I have enough issues of conscience I have yet to conquer.

It is wise to fear the Lord both with a sense of reverence and in the literal sense. For if we do not have fear of the Lord in the literal sense, we would be prone to dismiss the coming Judgment and be less thankful for the Grace extended to us to escape that awful event. *The Author*

Romans 15-16

Taking the Lead

God receives both strong and weak believers. Can we do less? God does not receive non-believers, He judges them!

Chapter 15 is a continuation of chapter fourteen on the subject of relationships within the Body of Christ. Perhaps an illustration helps us understand the Spirit Paul is making concerning not pleasing ourselves. Don't invite a Christian over for dinner you know doesn't drink and then set a glass of wine at his table setting. Or don't invite a Christian couple over who don't believe in dancing and once there, you and your wife put on a recording of 'Dancing in the Dark.'

Read Romans 15:1-6

1) Do you believe that being a strong Christian is based on biblical knowledge, excellent church attendance or character? Explain:

2) In your words, what qualities might be missing in a baby Christian? (See Overview)

3) What does it mean to be of good character, being Christ-like if you will? See John 8:29 and Matthew 3:17

4) The key word in verse one is *bear*. Which two of the following nine attributes of the *fruit of the spirit* is most needed from the mature Christian in dealing with an immature Christian? *"Love, joy, peace, patience, kindness, goodness, faithfulness, gentleness and self-control"* (Galatians 5:22)

Read Romans 15:7-22

5) It is important to correctly answer these two questions. Who did Christ come to minister to? See Matthew 2:6, 15:24 and Micah 5:2 – Who was the Apostle Paul sent to minister? (vv. 15-16) See also Acts 9:15.

6) What was Paul's priority? (vv. 20-21)

7) What explanation does Paul give for not yet having visited Rome? (vv. 17:22)

Read Romans 15:23-33

8) In visiting Rome at a future time, where else does Paul plan to visit? (vv. 23-24)

Summary Statement for Romans 15

In Mercy, <u>Yahweh came to earth in the person of Christ Jesus to redeem Israel</u>. In that visit, mercy was extended to the Gentile world by means of the Church. Within this unique Body of believers, there are of all sorts of Christians. Be they weak or strong in their faith, God receives all of them.

Read Romans 16

9) Why might chapter sixteen be a great example that Christianity is relational as much as it is doctrinal?

10) From this list of thirty-five names, what conclusion can we draw about Paul? See also Galatians 3:28 for additional insight.

Discussion:

Phoebe delivers Paul's letter to the Roman Church. Why do you think Paul sent his letter with a woman rather than a man? We offer two possible reasons: to test the Roman Christian's reception of her; to reinforce Galatians 3:28. What do you think?

11) Looking back to the Discussion topic of the 80/20 rule following question three in Romans 14, what is the peril of the eighty percent? See Revelation 2:4-5, 3:15-16

Discussion:

Circumcision was as divisive in the early Church as Denominationalism, women in the pulpit and musical styles are today. In addition to these three, some churches sprinkle, some immerse. Some perform same-sex-marriages, others vigorously oppose homosexual marriage. How much of all this do you think is more a matter of personal appetites and not so much Doctrinal truth?

Summary Statement for Romans 16

In addition to victory over death, the Cross is a symbol of the Ten Commandments.

The vertical wood on which the Lord's feet were nailed represents from head to toe, *love for God*. The horizontal wood on which the Lord's hands were nailed represents loving hands extended to *all men* around the world.

Paul declares that the strong in the Faith glorify God in ways the weak are not yet equipped to do. Think if you will, a second year piano student cannot perform as a seasoned pianist. Still, both can be received into membership of a piano guild.

The fruit of the Spirit comes naturally for the mature Christian. Before that, there is no magic bullet to maturity. <u>The moment we are saved, we simply change to whom we belong</u>. Maturity itself is a lifelong process directly related to how much of ourselves we are willing to surrender and our understanding of Grace.

Some baby Christians give the appearance of maturity because they impose upon themselves <u>their own list</u> of dos and don'ts to help God justify them. Little do they realize, they are literally glorifying self rather than God by their performance of these self-denials. If you are such a person, it is time to learn God is glorified by <u>His list</u> of dos; *"love, joy, peace, patience, kindness, goodness, faithfulness, gentleness and self-control."* (Galatians 6:22-23)

Backsliding is a pennant for another kind of baby Christian. This is usually the result of a failure to put on the full armor of God along the way. When backsliding occurs, we can be certain, the Spirit is grieved. Paul warns all Christians not to be a cause of the failures of other believers. This is why <u>Christians in positions of prominence must be alert to being used by Satan to corrupt God's people</u>. A microphone in odious hands is the devil's delight.

We probably have all had our do and don't issues at some point until we learned that <u>these simply are a matter of conscience</u> and not a matter of requirements for Justification. Maturity can be summed up in two axioms of the Christian Faith, the *Fruit of the Spirit* and the *Full Armor of God*.

There is a third quality of a mature Christian. Possessing the wisdom to identify <u>wolves in sheep's clothing</u>, false teachers, dividers and pretenders if you will. (Romans 16:17-19) In short, a mature Christian is neither naïve or confused about truth!

It is noteworthy that Paul names thirty-five people to conclude the Epistle. The list is inclusive of Jews and Gentiles, relatives and non-relatives, men and women. <u>Their</u>

names are forever etched in the annuals of Christianity. With two women topping the list, we are reminded that it was a woman through whom Christ came to earth.

The great Doctrines Paul proclaimed didn't arrive in the western world by leaflets from the sky or even a burning bush. The deliverer of this "Magna Carta of Christianity" wore shoes, heels in fact!

The rumor that Paul had little regard for women is eradicated in this chapter. Unfortunately, the Bible has been used against women for centuries by both men and the Church. To illustrate the misuse of the Word of God, a distraught Christian women confided to her pastor her husband was beating her. To which he replied, "If your husband kills you, it will be to the glory of God."

The stereotyping of women and suppressing them often rests on 1 Timothy 2:11-14. But we must remember, Timothy pastored in Ephesus, a place where the massive Temple of Diana had been ingrained into the culture for centuries. The priority of spreading the Gospel was too urgent to be lost in either political or cultural debates.

Let us hope that responsible Christian institutions are recognizing Scriptures is about all people, women included, in regard to gifting and structure accordingly.

Application

Christianity is centered in relationships! First with God, second with other believers and thirdly, with the lost. God choose Paul because he was a relentless personality; one dedicated to whatever his passion. He was not ego centered in that, he was quick to credit God and other people. This is the quality of a Christian. Paul demonstrated he had the passion to spread the Gospel. Can we demonstrate any less?

Notes for Romans 15-16

Romans 9
Israel, God's Sovereign Choice

Paul delivers a prayer-like introduction that reveals his anguish over Israel's rejection of its Messiah. (vv. 1-5) What God has conferred on this tiny nation, considering it is surrounded by hordes of enemies, leaves no doubt Israel is God's chosen people.

1) Underline in your Bible and name the seven penchants plus the one additional one God has conferred upon Israel. (vv. 4-5) See the Summary Statement for assistance.

2) Why do you think God choose Israel? (vv. 1-5) Why not chose a powerful empire like Rome to bring such a magnificent King to earth? Why do you think the birth of Jesus was first announced to shepherds in the field and not to the elite religious community in Jerusalem? (Luke 2:8-15)

3) Are all Jews Abraham's children? _____ (v. 8)

4) From this lengthy in-depth account by Paul, what are some conclusions you can draw on the subject of election? (vv. 8-26)

Discussion:

Without reading ahead to chapters ten and eleven, Paul would seem to be saying that Israel is hopelessly lost and God has selected the Gentiles as His chosen people. What do you say, and on what do you base your reasoning? (Consider vv. 1-5)

Romans 10
Israel's Rejection

Israel had lived by the Law since the time of Moses. But to the last man, <u>all had failed</u>. To this day, Israel rejects the idea of Faith, choosing to remain under the Law. But like those before them, they fall short of fulfilling the letter of the Law. (Ecclesiastes 7:20) Christ came and fulfilled it for them (Matthew 5:17, 20) But still, they remain obstinate.

5) How does Paul explain Israel's actions and what is so different about a life lived by Faith and a life lived by Law? (vv. 1-5)

6) What is Paul's message in verses nine through eleven?

7) What is Paul's point in verses twelve and thirteen?

8) What is necessary to get the Gospel out to the whole world? (vv. 14-15)

9) What was Paul's and Steven's experience when they tried to bring the good news to Israel and the surrounding nations? See Acts 7:51-60, 16:22-24, 17:13, 19:26-31

Romans 11
Restoration Solves a Mystery

<u>The inclusion of the Gentile Church is not an abandonment of Israel</u>. To the contrary, the two shall be united to the same root, the olive tree of Christ. (v. 17)

10) White-Supremacists and even some main-stream Christians believe that God is through with Israel. But what do the Scriptures say? (vv. 1-5, 11-12) See also Revelation 7:3-8, 12:1-6, 14:1, 21:2, 14

11) What was the primary purpose Israel was hardened? (vv. 8-12)

12) What is Paul's message to the Church? (vv. 17-21)

13) What is the hope for Israel in the future? (vv. 22-24, 28-29)

14) Many love to predict the Coming of Christ by events on earth. But what do the Scriptures reveal will determine Christ's return? (v. 25) See also Revelation 6:10-11

Summary Statement:

Israel was given much: Adoption (As sons), Glory (Shekinah Glory), Covenants (The bonds), The Law (God's plumb-line), A Kingdom of Priests (Worship leading), Promises (To see them through battles and beyond), and Fathers (Abraham, Isaac and Jacob), and finally Christ. By these initiations, Salvation has come to the Gentiles!

 **Leader's Helicopter Overview of Romans 9-11**
(Optional or Prepare Your Own)

These three chapters are appendages of Christian Doctrine and are covered here as a single lesson. <u>How this section is studied is discretionary but it must be studied</u>! Because the root of Christianity rests on Israel as outlined in these three chapters.

Paul acknowledges Israel's stumble. For a time, it seems God is through with Israel and replaced her with the Church. Paul grieves over Israel's rejection of Jesus but still, he does not lose sight of God's end plan.

For election enthusiasts, this is your lesson. Election is one of the debatable topics among Christians. <u>Election is about position</u>. On earth, the elected are positioned for service. So too, newborns of the Spirit are repositioned to a son-ship with Christ. The position of belonging to the world changes to belonging to God<u>.</u>

Psalm 69:28 and Revelation 3:5 indicate at the moment we become a life-form in our mother's womb, we are entered into the Book of Life. (If this is not so, then the anti-abortionists have no case.) But <u>physical life is a result of natural conception</u>. If during the age of accountability a supernatural new birth has not taken place, what was born of the flesh is blotted out of the Book of Life. The person was never born-again. Now the tricky part. Why was Esau out of favor with God? He was the first twin to come out! Or still, <u>what had Jacob done to be in God's favor?</u> In fact, Jacob was the second twin born! With no works credited to either, was God being unfair? – No, God was being Sovereign! <u>We do not know God's purpose</u>. To question it would be treasonous. One conclusion to consider is the concept of the First shall be last and the Last shall be First. We will not attempt this subject further other than to say, election and freewill are both valid.

We are told the Jews were zealous for God but still remained lost. They failed to understand that <u>Heaven only accepts God's righteousness</u>. Many today believe if they are sincere in whatever they believe, or if they are a good person, Heaven will receive them. Beloved, <u>that is the most dangerous blunder a person will ever make</u>.

There is a reference to the Rapture in Romans 11:25-27. Many, if not most <u>Christians believe the *myth* that events on earth</u> will determine Christ's return. They believe worldwide acceptance of same-sex-marriage, removal of *in God we trust* from the dollar bill or a society resembling Sodom and Gomorrah will serve as catalysts for God shutting down the world. "See what the world is coming to" people say! Beloved, the world has already come to it! Just for starters, consider horrendous events such as Hitler's murder of six million Jews or Stalin murdering twenty-million of his own people. The carnage in the Pacific war killed millions more. World War II netted fifty-million people dead. Gun deaths in the U. S. is epidemic. Lawlessness, selfishness, narcissism, uncommitted hearts shacking-up and today's technological age makes pornography as close as one's computer. Our sex crazed society is without precedent and that is saying a lot considering the world's history.

As horrendous as are these events, the truth of when Christ returns is not based on events on earth. *These are only the signs.* The end is based on events completed in Heaven! Romans 11:25, Revelation 6:1-11, 12:7-12 Until X number of Gentiles are brought in, the war raging even now in the heavens continues for souls on a scale you and I can't comprehend. The final battle of Armageddon will encompass both earth and the heavens. What follows after those events will fulfill the last of God's Covenants with Israel. Following Israel's Redemption, there will be a coming together of Jews and Gentiles which is the mystery Paul identifies in Romans 11:25.

Application

In a world awash in pluralisms and secular promptings, what plans have you made?

Notes for Romans 9, 10, 11

Of those who serve the Lord it is said:

The

Lord redeems

His servants.

No one

Will be condemned

Who takes refuge

In Him.

Psalm 34:22

Blessed are they who wash their robes

That they may have the right

To the tree of life.

And may go through the gates

Into the city.

I am the Alpha and the Omega

The First and the Last

The Beginning and the End.

Concluding Dissertation

"Who may ascend the hill of the Lord? Who may stand in his holy place?"
"He who has clean hands and a pure heart, <u>who does not swear by what is false</u>."
Psalm 24:3-4

Listening to the Wrong Voices

Sampson listened to the wrong people and it got the better of him. Eve listened to just one wrong voice and it got the better of us all. There are voices today robbing people of Kingdom living. These voices get rich from inflicting fear and paranoia in the minds of people, even Christians. <u>It is not Christian to live in fear</u>! These voices deceive the vulnerable to trust favored mortals more than God. Faith is weakened when fear seizes the mind. The Bible overwhelmingly refutes fear in too many places to list. Fear pulls the rug from under love. <u>For who can love one whom they fear</u>? Franklin Roosevelt said of fear, "The only thing we have to fear is fear itself."

<u>The world considers truth optional</u>. From within and from without, compelling voices drive our decision-making. Within are the voices of our appetites, emotions, biases, desires, ambitions and yes, even laziness, all cutting paths for us to follow. From without are television, radio, newsprint, influential personalities, pastors, teachers, friends, circumstances and all manner of worldly enticements. A maze of voices, all having one purpose, to influence our decisions that ultimately take us down a path. <u>The wise will take self out of the picture and put God in the picture</u>.

Glorifying God rather than self is the safest decision one can make! When God's Laws are remembered, we are assured of <u>avoiding sin's destructive paths</u>. God has a plan for our life but then, so does the devil. Remember Jesus' words to Peter; *"Satan has asked to sift you as wheat, but I have prayed for you that your faith may not fail."* (Luke 22:31-32)

When we flip on the television or the radio, where the dial comes to rest is determined by our appetite. Some have an appetite for satisfying their itching ears while others have an <u>appetite for truth</u>. Itching ears are fertile ground for liars and deceivers. Some channels broadcast news. Others appeal to our scientific natures. Most channels however, are designed simply to pass the time with the mundane. Their content is quickly forgotten and have little influence. For the most part, these time-passers pose no threat to sending anyone down sin's destructive path.

There are conspiracy-theory voices bent on <u>dividing people</u> and scaring the daylights out of them, especially Christians. *Me thinks* people dial them up for the same reason kids attend Frankenstein movies. Truthfully, Frankenstein is more believable! Attempts to identify with Christian tenets might just stick with these networks were it not for contradictory leggy blond starlets making stuff up from behind frontless news desks. These are among the throngs of false prophets of which the Bible warns.

Fear and conspiracy commentators are clouds without rain. The sky will fall if their man isn't elected. Beloved, the sky will fall when God determines it to fall! We recall the prophecies of these clouds without rain following the 2008 elections. Gestapo type government would plunge the nation into an abyss they warned. There would be no more presidential elections! Antichrist had come they screamed! Beloved, none of this occurred. These voices of doom just harped on a subject until you just wanted to scream. Still, people listened to them. *"You will know them by their fruit."* (Matthew 7:16 NKJV) Oh how these voices love to argue! Strife and quarreling are pervasive with those whose faith is weak and top the list of things the Lord *detests.* (Proverbs 10:12; 2 Timothy 2:23-25; James 4:1)

Some falsely believe they can serve the greater good by compromising the truth. That is demonic deception. It is not unusual to see on camera, groups of people assembled directly behind a speaker <u>affirming a blatant lie</u>. Some of these folks are Christians. The Kingdom of God will not be built on fear, character assassinations, lies and deception. Beloved, political races are the devil's playground and a game of roulette robbing many of the coming Kingdom. And they don't even know it.

> *"Not everyone who says to me, 'Lord, Lord,' will enter the kingdom of heaven,*
> *But only he who does the will of my Father who is in heaven."*
> *"Many will say to me on that day, 'Lord, Lord, did we not prophesy in you name*
> *And perform many miracles?" "Then I will tell them plainly,*
> *'I never knew you. Away from me, you evildoers!"*
> **Matthew 7:21-23**

Whether sitting at our computer, engaged in conversation or responding to circumstances, to whom we listen <u>influence our choices that determine our destiny</u>.

> *"Whatever is true, whatever is noble, whatever is right,*
> *whatever is pure, whatever is lovely, whatever is admirable,*
> *if anything is excellent or praiseworthy – think on these things."*
> **Philippians 4:8**

Prayer is a Holy Thing

The things of God are Holy. Prayer is a precious and Holy thing because it is one-on-one Communion with our Lord. One person in our class said she gets discouraged because it seems as if God never answers her prayers. She is not alone in that thinking. But many things come into play regarding prayer. First, prayer is a statement of belief which is no small thing. Praying says something of us and something we can take comfort in. Praying draws us closer to God more than any other medium. Prayer offers us the means to lose ourselves to Him which is far more important than things granted. As far as prayers being answered, not answered or delayed, there are excellent writers out there from which we can draw insight from.

Certainly all the people identified in Hebrews 11:32-39 were prayer warriors but still, for many, their life ended tragically. The answer to why God didn't answer their prayers for reprieve lay in the very next verse, God had something better for them.

1 John 5:16 suggests there are people out of the reach of prayer. Obviously this would include all unbelievers and believers out of the will of God. We do not find one prayer in the Book of Esther and for good reason. The Hebrews who did not return from the land of idol worshiping Babylon and Persia were out of the will of God. What saved those people from annihilation was the Mercy and Providence of God. That circumstance happens today when without petition, the Lord looks after all of us including unbelievers. For God wishes that no one perishes. (2 Peter 3:9)

However, Christians praying for God to grant goodies to an unbeliever, loved one or friend, to get a promotion is an affront to the purpose and holiness of prayer. God reserved prayer for His people! Jesus said as much when He said, *"Do not give what is holy to dogs, nor cast your pearls before swine."* (Matthew 7:6) Anyone living apart from the Son is not of the family of God. So let us not disgrace prayer with petitions for individuals estranged from the Father. The only prayer we should offer on behalf of an unbelieving loved one or friend is for their Salvation. Good things do come to unbelievers but not because of prayer. God grants them good fortune to give them reason to see Him! For example, when the rich man dies apart from God, he will be held accountable for not having given God all the praise for his affluent life.

Evangelist Billy Graham's reply when asked if he had any regrets regarding his Christian life was one most Christians might consider about themselves. He said his prayer life was not what it should have been. Certainly this writer can relate.

The Worship Service is a Holy Assembly

Hallowed Be Thy Name

Sometimes it seems as if Christians think being saved is a casual thing because of the ease one is saved. *"For my yoke is easy and my burden is light."* (Matthew 11:30) Perhaps such a relaxed mind-set leads many to think nothing of carrying food and drink into a worship service or wearing shorts and sandals to church. Some churches advertise coming casual. One must wonder which of the seven churches in the Book of Revelation they wish to be identified. What a crass way to honor the Creator of all things and the One who suffered on our behalf. How inconsiderate to crawl over worshipers during a closing prayer to get an early start to the parking lot.

Certainly church attire is a slippery slope. <u>So let us address it as one of attitude rather than of requirement.</u> We are aware of the misgivings of James 2:2-4 and the dress of Jesus and his disciples. Still, it is important that our image of God is that of a Holy God and not simply a casual man upstairs sipping an icy.

But really, how casual should God be approached in corporate worship? The priests washed their hands before entering the holy of holies. Men sacrificed <u>their best</u> animal before the Lord. Consider the following Scriptures. *"Take off your sandals, for the place you are standing is holy ground."* (Exodus 3:5, Joshua 5:15) *"They will walk with me dressed in white."* (Revelation 3:4) *"A woman must not wear men's clothing, nor a man wear women's clothing, for the Lord your God detests anyone who does this."* (Deuteronomy 22:5) *"Then out came a woman to meet him, dressed like a prostitute"* (Proverbs 7:10) In all cases, appearance delivered a message. Are we to dismiss these Scriptures as simply dated symbolism? <u>Did the Cross make God less Holy</u>?

What we wear says a lot about our attitude before our God. We should never forget, He is King of Kings and Lord of Lords! When we gather as a body before the Lord, folks, we are coming before Him as a <u>Bride betrothed to Him</u>! Citing Jesus chastisement of the Pharisee's religious clothing is an empty defense of appearing slovenly for worship because it was not about the clothing. <u>It was about the hypocrisy beneath the clothing</u>. So please, let us not use the Pharisees to justify shabbiness. Ruth prepared herself for Boaz. Should we do less? "Come just as you are" is in reference to Christ receiving us in spite of our sin and has nothing to do with <u>being cavalier in our approach to corporate worship</u>.

Oswald Chamber's book 'My Utmost for His Highest' doesn't center on what we wear to church. But it certainly is suggestive of <u>honor befitting a King</u>. What we wear to a worship service reflects our mind set to those around us. Once we have been washed in the blood of the Lamb, don't we have a responsibility to appear washed, not just inside, but outside also? As for me and my house, we will wear our best, do our best, and pray my heart matches my tie.

John Pennington

"The eyes of the Lord are on the righteous,
and his ears are attentive to their cry."
Psalm 34:15

Printed in the United States
By Bookmasters